D1798231

THE MOUNTAINS OF ENGLAND AND WALES

THE REFERENCE LIBRARY

GENERAL EDITOR: Louis C. Baume

THE COUNTRY CODE

Fasten all gates

Guard against all risk of fire

Keep dogs under control

Keep to paths across farm land

Avoid damaging fences, hedges and walls

Leave no litter

Safeguard water supplies

Protect wild life, wild plants and trees

Go carefully on country roads

Respect the life of the countryside

Great Gable from Lingmell

THE MOUNTAINS OF ENGLAND AND WALES

TABLES OF MOUNTAINS OF TWO THOUSAND FEET
AND MORE IN ALTITUDE

George Bridge

Photographs by W. A. Poucher, FRPS

Maps by George Bridge

Gaston's Alpine Books
West Col Productions

First published in Great Britain jointly by
Gaston's Alpine Books and West Col Productions
1 Meadow Close, Goring, Reading, Berks. RG8 OAP

By the same author
<u>Rock Climbing in the British Isles 1894-1970</u>

<u>Acknowledgements</u>

My thanks are owed to Mr. W. A. Poucher, F. R. P. S. whose
camera studies grace this book, and whose wonderful
photographs have delighted several generations of mountain-
lovers.

I must also thank the staffs of the Ordnance Survey Office,
Southampton, of the British Museum Library and Map Room,
and of the Manchester Central Reference Library for their
invaluable help, and Robin G. Collomb and Louis C. Baume
for their encouragement and patience.

Olivetti Editor 5C setting and camera copy
preparation by West Col Productions

Printed in England by Cox & Wyman Ltd.,
London, Fakenham, Reading

CONTENTS

Editor's Preface	10
Introduction	11
Table 1: Mountains in Regional Groups	16
Notes to Table 1	21
LAKE DISTRICT	27
High Street Group	30
Helvellyn Group	36
Skiddaw Group	42
Buttermere Group	46
Great Gable Group	48
Scafell Group	54
Coniston Group	58
THE CHEVIOTS	61
THE PENNINES	67
Northern Pennines	67
Black Fell Group	70
Burnhope Seat Group	72
Cross Fell Group	74
Central Pennines	77
Great Shunner Group	80
Ingleborough Group	84
Southern Pennines	88
Peak District	88
DARTMOOR	92
ISLE OF MAN	94
WALES	96
North Wales	96
The Carneddau	100
The Glyders	102

Snowdon Group   106

Moel Hebog Group   108

Moel Siabod Group   110

The Arennigs   116

The Berwyns   118

The Arans   122

The Rhinogs   126

Cader Idris Group   128

Central Wales   131

Pumlumon   134

Rhayader Mountains   134

Radnor Forest   136

South Wales   139

Brecon Beacons   142

Black Mountains   146

Table 2: Mountains in order of Altitude   148

Table 3: Mountains in Alphabetical Order   160

Table 4: The County Tops of England and Wales   175

Bibliography   186

Glossary of Welsh Mountain Names   190

Reader's Logbook   200

MAPS

The Mountains of England and Wales — 8/9
Lake District Mountains — 24/25
High Street Group — 28/29
Helvellyn Group — 34/35
Skiddaw and Coniston Groups — 40/41
Buttermere and Great Gable Groups — 44/45
Scafell Group — 52/53
The Cheviots — 62/63
Northern Pennines — 68/69
Central Pennines — 78/79
Peak District and Dartmoor — 90/91
The Carneddau and Glyders — 98/99
Snowdon, Moel Hebog and Moel Siabod Groups — 104/105
The Arennigs, Berwyns and Arans — 114/115
The Rhinogs and Cader Idris Group — 124/125
Central Wales — 132/133
South Wales — 140/141
County Tops of England and Wales — 176/177

ILLUSTRATIONS

Great Gable from Lingmell — frontis.
Blencathra from Great Gable — 27
Striding Edge and Helvellyn — 39
Pillar Fell from the Wastwater Hotel — 51
Scafell Range seen up Eskdale — 57
Langdale Pikes from Elterwater Village — 50
Ingleborough from the North — 77
Snowdon from Llyn Llydaw — 97
Lliwedd , Snowdon, Crib-y-ddysgl and Crib-goch — 112
Cader Idris from the North — 113
Pen-y-Fan, Brecon Beacons — 139

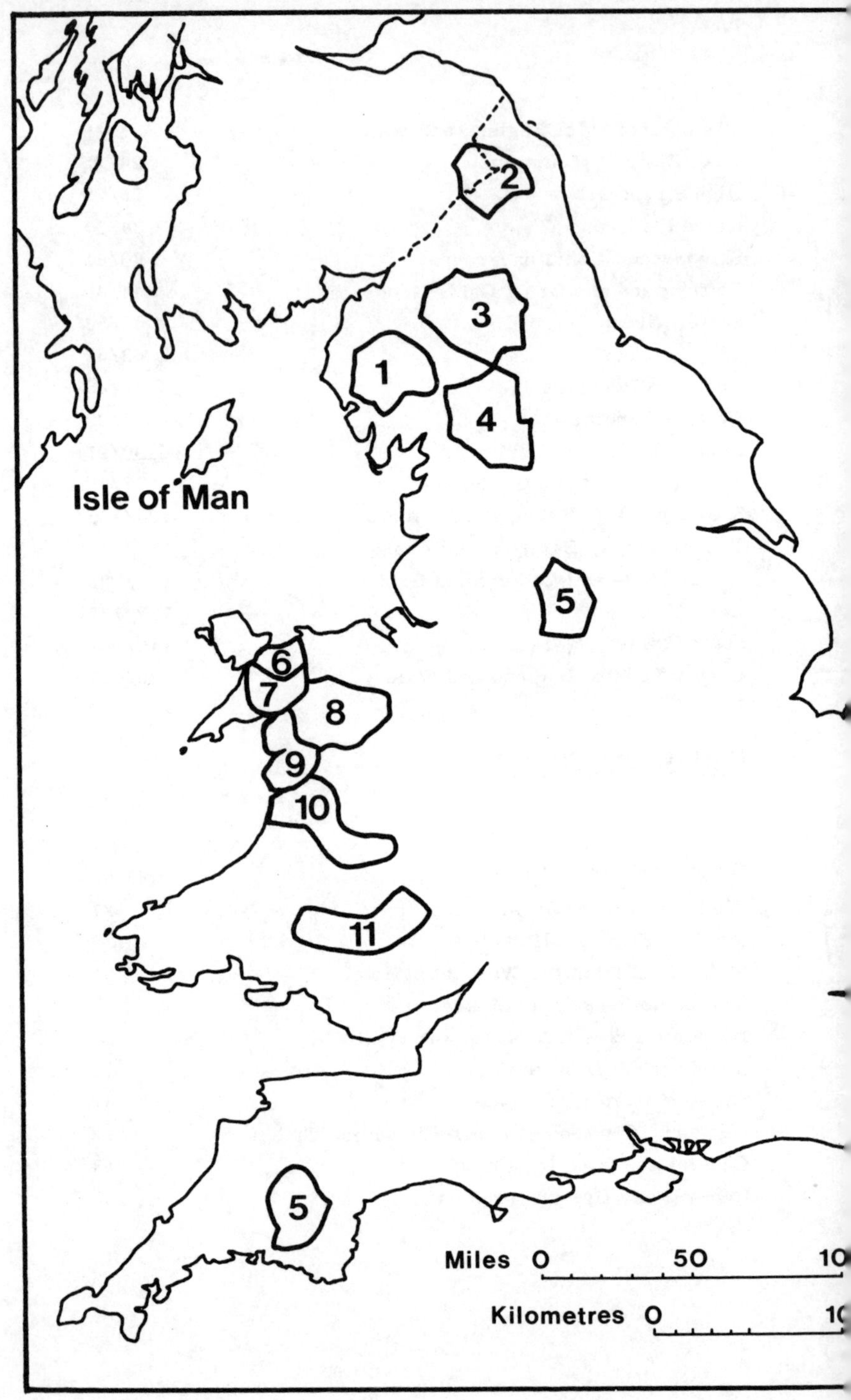

Isle of Man
1
2
3
4
5
6
7
8
9
10
11
5
Miles 0 50 10
Kilometres 0 10

KEY TO MAPS

1 Lake District
2 The Cheviots
3 Northern Pennines
4 Central Pennines
5 Peak District and Dartmoor
6 Carneddau and Glyders
7 Snowdon, Moel Hebog and Moel Siabod Groups
8 The Arennigs, Berwyns and Arans
9 The Rhinogs and Cader Idris
10 Central Wales (Pumlumon, Rhayader Mountains
    and Radnor Forest)
11 Brecon Beacons and Black Mountains

THE MOUNTAINS
OF ENGLAND AND WALES

EDITOR'S PREFACE

Eighty years ago, Munro first published his Tables of the Mountains of Scotland. It is surprising that - except for the pioneering efforts of Corbett, Docharty and others which, privately printed or published in Club Journals, were not available to the general public - nothing similar has ever appeared for the mountains 'south of the Border'; and this despite that fact that, as this present work shows, there are more than 400 Tops of 2000 feet and over. All the hard work involved in the compilation of these Tables (the first volume to appear in our Reference Library series) has been undertaken most painstakingly and meticulously by George Bridge. In addition to a vast amount of research work, this has entailed the actual ascents of a great number of tops for the verification of finer details 'in situ': no mean enterprise on the part of the author to whom we acknowledge our gratitude. The maps have been drawn by him, also, and these should make easy the quick identification of peaks and their relative positions. The photographic illustrations, depicting the great variety and poetic splendour of our hills and mountains, are the work of W. A. Poucher F. R. P. S.

In planning this work we decided to show heights in metres as well as in feet in order to comply with the gradual adoption of the metric system.   Distances, however, are given in miles only (even though the Grid system itself is metric) because to show both would have resulted in a very confusing and repetitious lay-out. In any case, the relevant scales in miles and in metres appear at the bottom of all Ordnance Survey maps.

Everything changes: the heights of mountains are modified, and County boundaries altered; it has even been prophesied that the mountains and hills shall be made low. In the meantime, any additional information or corrections relevant to the context of this work will be welcomed by myself or the author.

Louis Baume

INTRODUCTION

The first mountaineer in the British Isles to take up the idea of ascending all
the mountains above a certain height was Hugh (later Sir Hugh) T. Munro.
His <u>Tables of the 3000-Feet Mountains of Scotland</u> was published in 1891 and
rapidly became famous as the mountaineer's handbook to that country. It has
since gone through several editions and many printings. Munro himself suc-
ceeded in climbing all but two of the mountains before his death in 1919.
Soon after the appearance of the Munro's <u>Tables</u>, a Manchester mountaineer
by the name of P.S. Minor conceived the plan of ascending all the mountains
above 2500 feet in England and Wales. This lower height was chosen because
the two countries possess too few mountains of over 3000-foot altitude to offer
enough of a challenge. When he began to approach the end of this task it occur-
red to some younger members of his club - that is, the Rucksack Club - to
"make sure that he did it properly". The appropriate sheets of the Ordnance
Survey One Inch Map were diligently searched for fresh mountains and the
outcome was the list which J. Rooke Corbett assembled for the Rucksack Club
Journal in 1911. Their total of "Twenty-Fives", as they called them, was 131.
During the next few years many other club members besides Minor visited all
these mountains, and the publication in the middle twenties of a new and better
series of maps - the "Popular" Edition of the One Inch - made necessary a
revision of the list in 1929. (It is worth noting at this point that Munro's
Tables had been from the beginning based on information taken from the O.S.
Six Inch Map. Rooke Corbett's lists were dependent on a rather artificial
convention, the mountains detectable on the One Inch scale.) Rooke Corbett's
new list of "Twenty-Fives" gave details of 148 mountains. As a humorous
aside he noted that one other mountain, Gallt yr Ogof (in the Glyders group,
North Wales) fell short of the magic figure and rose to only 2499 feet. "After
much discussion," writes Rooke Corbett, "it was agreed that this peak might
be counted as a twenty-five by any climber who, when standing on the topmost

summit, leaped at least one foot into the air." It is not known how many climbers took advantage of this dispensation.

The next list of this kind to be compiled was that of "all the points in England of two-thousand feet and over" by the Rev. W.T. Elmslie in 1933. It was based on the height indicators printed on the Bartholomew Half Inch Maps, which were, and are still, contoured at only 250-foot intervals. Furthermore Elmslie's list was, as he makes plain himself, a personal one; he was not exclusively concerned with mountain summits as such, only with points given definite height value on the map. A great many of his "two-thousand-footers" were merely spot heights on rising hillsides, often with nothing to identify them exactly on the ground. Elmslie's list, inflated as it was with spot heights, contained 347 entries.

The idea of climbing all the mountains above this new level of two thousand feet had now taken a firm hold, and things could obviously not long be left at that. The first improved list of a limited group of the English mountains formed part of an elegant essay on the Lake District mountains by F.H.F. Simpson in 1937; and as a result of E. Moss's efforts the list was extended to the rest of the English mountains in 1939, and to Wales in 1940. Both men made extensive use of the Six Inch series of maps and their combined lists of the mountains of the two countries then totalled 612 entries. A few years later Moss managed to bring to light a few hitherto overlooked mountains, and the final figure rose to 621 mountains.

In 1954 W. McKnight Docharty, an ardent mountain-lover if ever there was one, issued a massive volume describing his ascents of mountains in the British Isles and listing 900 of them. The majority of the mountains in Docharty's lists were of 2500 feet or more in altitude though he rather arbitrarily included many others of lesser height. In the two supplementary volumes which followed in 1962 he extended his lists to include most of the mountains above 2000 feet, and again he listed a great many others of lesser altitude.

In all of these lists except Elmslie's, the qualifying feature required for a listing was stated to be the possession of at least one contour ring as shown on the Ordnance Survey One Inch Map, this map being of course contoured at fifty-foot intervals. However, as has been pointed out at intervals all along, the presence or absence of a single contour ring does not necessarily tell us very much about the separateness of a given mountain. The presence of a single contour ring may result in the inclusion in the lists of a quite minor protuberance, while the absence of such a contour may result in the exclusion of a more prominent feature of much greater rise from lower ground all round. A rise of a mere five feet at the right altitude can generate a contour ring on the map, while elsewhere a rise of more than forty-five feet can fail to do so, because the whole of the rise takes place between the contour levels. All the lists mentioned above suffer from this or from other anomalies.

In the present book an attempt has been made to deal with this problem by requiring each listed mountain (or "top") to be separated from all the others by a real rise of fifty feet or more all round. The best evidence for this is usually the Ordnance Survey Six Inch Map, supplemented where necessary by maps at other scales. The information printed on these maps includes, in order of usefulness, the height values assigned to triangulation stations, bench marks, spot heights and contours. Other sources of information have been used, including direct information from the Ordnance Survey and, where all else failed, observations made by amateur surveyors. As explained in more detail in the Notes to Table 1, the Ordnance Survey is in process of changing the height values of certain mountain summits for reasons which include revisions due to new surveys, and the policy of indicating only the triangulation station height values where these differ from the highest (summit) ground-level height values and where no room can be found on the maps for both. The latest available information has been used for this book and only slight changes are expected in the future.

A very useful distinction made by Munro in his lists of the Scottish mountains has been employed here also, and that is the distinction between "separate mountains" and their "subsidiary mountains". No definition of the difference between these two classes of mountains was ever laid down by Munro, though his topographical knowledge of Scotland and his feeling for mountain structure won for his lists a wide measure of acceptance among mountaineers. In a study of the Scottish highlands this position is reasonable enough. The mountains of Scotland are generally regarded as the remains of an approximately 3000-foot high tableland heavily dissected into the form we now see, and a division of the resultant mountains into "separate" and "subsidiary" mountains is comparatively easy and unambiguous to make, without requiring a very explicit explanation of the difference between them.

With the mountains of England and Wales this is not the case. There has been no raised tableland of any height from which all the mountains have been carved, and the origins of the elevation of English and Welsh mountains admit of no single explanation. It has been found necessary therefore to define the two classes of mountains more closely. The topographical feature that separates neighbouring mountains may be either a valley or a col (or pass). In the case of a valley separating two mountains, no difficulty in deciding their status usually arises. In that of an intervening col it may be a very different matter. Clearly, height differences between the level of the col and those of the respective mountain summits are not sufficient by themselves to establish "separateness" in the required sense. A height difference of (for instance) a hundred

feet might reasonably establish separateness between mountains far apart:
it could hardly do so for two mountains close together. It follows that the
height qualification must be coupled with a "distance-apart" qualification.
In this book, in order to merit separate status, mountains close together are
required to share a much deeper col than mountains farther apart, bearing in
mind that the distance apart is to be measured not in a straight line but following the convolutions of the highest connecting ridge.

The definition adopted here for a <u>Separate Mountain</u> is: a mountain of an
altitude of 2000 feet or more which is separated from all other separate mountains in the list by a height difference above any intervening cols of at least
500 feet at half a mile apart, 250 feet at one mile apart, 100 feet at two miles
apart, and pro rata. Diagram 1 shows the curve which defines the minimum
qualification for separate mountains. Above the curve will be found the qualifying co-ordinates for all separate mountains; below it those of all subsidiary
mountains. It is worth noting that beyond four miles all mountains of greater
than fifty-foot rise all round are reckoned as separate mountains.

<u>Subsidiary Mountains</u> are defined as mountains of an altitude of 2000 feet or
more which are separated from all other mountains in the list by a height
difference above any intervening cols of fifty feet or more but which do not
qualify as separate mountains as defined above. Diagram 2 represents the
profile of three mountains, two of which, A and C, are separate mountains,
the crucial height differences A-B and B-C being greater than the required
minimum qualification at this distance. The other mountain represented, E,
is a subsidiary mountain, the height difference D-E being barely fifty feet.
As a final point, the reader is reminded that we are using the word "mountains"
(or "tops") in these Tables to mean any or all of the separate and the subsidiary
mountains in England and Wales; the two classes of "separate mountains" and
"subsidiary mountains" together comprise the "mountains" ("tops") of the
two countries.

It is believed that these definitions have resulted in the formation of a more
realistic list of the worthwhile mountains of England and Wales for the mountaineer. Every care has been taken to secure accuracy and completeness in
the Tables, and it is hoped that mistakes will not be found very numerous.

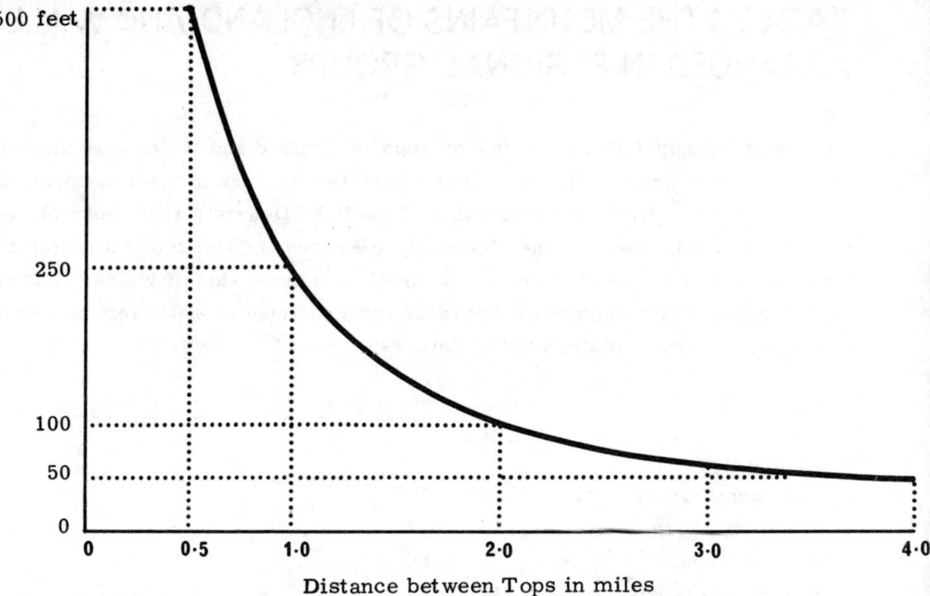

Diagram 1. Curve of minimum qualification for a Separate Mountain

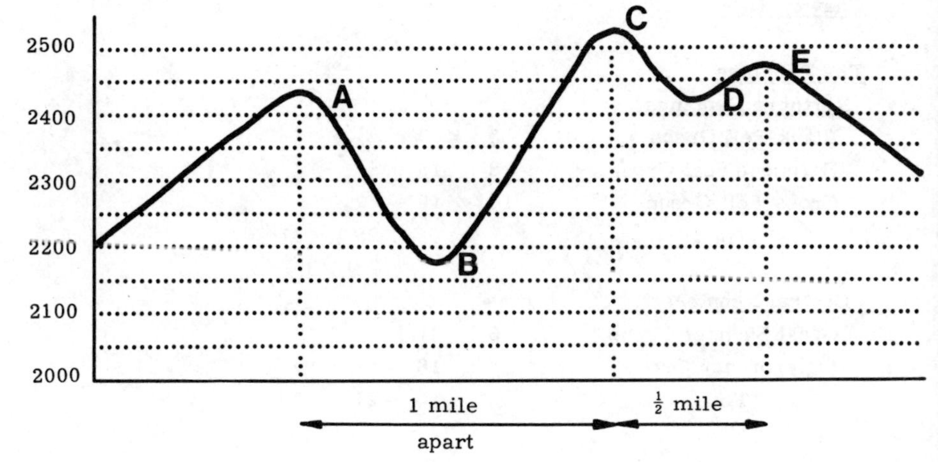

Diagram 2. Separate Mountains (A and C) and a Subsidiary Mountain (E)

TABLE 1 THE MOUNTAINS OF ENGLAND AND WALES ARRANGED IN REGIONAL GROUPS

The two-thousand-foot mountains or tops of England and Wales rise almost entirely in the north and west. It is convenient to think of them as forming three divisions: first, the mountains of the Lake District; then those of the rest of England, that is, the Cheviots, Pennines and Dartmoor (the Isle of Man also fits conveniently here); and finally the mountains of Wales. There are altogether 408 mountains or tops in the two countries of 2,000 feet or more in height. They are distributed as follows:

	Sep. Mtns.	Tops	s.m.	t.	s.m.	t.	s.m.	t.
Lake District								
High Street Group	10	23						
Helvellyn Group	13	27						
Skiddaw Group	8	18						
Buttermere Group	10	15						
Great Gable Group	15	27						
Scafell Group	12	29						
Coniston Group	6	11						
Total:					74	150		
Cheviot Hills					6	8		
The Pennines								
Northern Pennines								
Black Fell Group	3	3						
Burnhope Seat Group	8	15						
Cross Fell Group	14	19						
Total:			25	37				
Central Pennines								
Great Shunner Group	13	21						
Ingleborough Group	14	18						
Total:			27	39				
Southern Pennines								
Peak District	2	3						
Total:			2	3				
Total: The Pennines					54	79		

	Sep. Mtns.	Tops	s. m.	t.	s. m.	t.	s. m.	t.
Dartmoor					1	2		
Isle of Man					1	1		
Total: England							136	240

Wales

North Wales

	Sep. Mtns.	Tops	s. m.	t.
The Carneddau	12	17		
The Glyders	8	10		
Snowdon Group	8	10		
Moel Hebog Group	6	10		
Moel Siabod Group	9	11		
The Arennigs	8	11		
The Berwyns	10	21		
The Arans	8	14		
The Rhinogs	6	8		
Cader Idris Group	9	14		
Total:			84	126

Central Wales

	Sep. Mtns.	Tops	s. m.	t.
Pumlumon	3	4		
Rhayader Mountains	3	3		
Radnor Forest	2	4		
Total:			8	11

South Wales

	Sep. Mtns.	Tops	s. m.	t.
Brecon Beacons	13	19		
Black Mountains*	7	12		
Total:			20	31

	s. m.	t.
Total: Wales	112	168
Grand Total: England and Wales	248	408

*Two of the separate mountains in the Black Mountains are traversed by the boundary between Wales and England. However, they are more conveniently included here.

The southernmost two-thousander in England is High Willhays in Dartmoor; the northernmost is The Cheviot; the easternmost is Bleaklow Stones, the eastern summit of Bleaklow in the Peak District; and the westernmost is Snaefell in the Isle of Man, or, counting the mainland only, High Willhays again. In Wales the southernmost two-thousander is Cefn yr Ystrad in the Brecon Beacons; the northernmost is Tal y Fan in the Carneddau; the easternmost is Pen y Garn Fawr in the Black Mountains; and the westernmost is Garnedd-goch in the Moel Hebog Group. The two-thousanders of England with the Isle of Man extend farther than those of Wales in every direction. However, if only the mainland is considered, then Garnedd-goch (Moel Hebog Group) is the westernmost top in the two countries.

				Separate mtns.	tops
From 2000 feet to	2099 feet there are			45	85
2100	2199			34	59
2200	2299			34	61
2300	2399			30	43
2400	2499			20	32
2500	2599			19	29
2600	2699			16	26
2700	2799			11	21
2800	2899			9	16
2900	2999			12	15
3000	3099			5	8
3100	3199			5	5
3200	3299			4	4
3300	3399			0	0
3400	3499			3	3
3500	3560			1	1
Total, from 2000	3560			248	408

The two-thousand-foot tops of England and Wales are distributed among the following counties, many being situated on county boundaries and thus shared by two or, in one case, three counties.

	Separate Mtns.	tops
Brecknockshire	18	29
Caernarvonshire	39	52
Cardiganshire	3	4
Carmarthenshire	3	3
Cumberland	60	111
Denbighshire	7	13
Derbyshire	2	3
Devon	1	2
Durham	5	12
Hereford	2	2
Isle of Man	1	1
Lancashire	7	12
Merionethshire	44	69
Monmouthshire	2	2
Montgomeryshire	4	10
Northumberland	9	12
Radnorshire	2	4
Westmorland	36	74
Yorkshire, North Riding	13	18
Yorkshire, West Riding	15	23

The 408 two-thousanders of England and Wales are also distributed on the 230 "islands" of land which rise above the 2,000-foot contour; that is to say, supposing the sea level ever rose to that height (an event which few of us could contemplate with complete composure) there would be exactly so many real islands riding above the waves, at least temporarily. The largest new island so formed would be that of the Cross Fell group of mountains, and it would be eleven miles long. Few of the other islands would exceed six miles in length. It makes an interesting exercise for rainy days, identifying them all!

Many excellent walks and expeditions can be devised with the object of traversing several of these tops together in one or more days. The permutations are endless and quite beyond the scope of this book. The ultimate possibility is a continuous odyssey linking all 408 two-thousanders in one long expedition. As a rough guide (which can be employed as a whole or in its constituent parts) a determined mountaineer or hill-walker could probably achieve the whole series in the following times. The figures in brackets refer to additional days for rest and travelling between the mountain regions.

Cheviots	2	(1)
High Street Group	2	(1)
Helvellyn Group	2	(1)
Skiddaw Group	2	(1
Buttermere Group	2	
Great Gable Group	2	(1)
Scafell Group	3	(1)
Coniston Group	1	(1)
Northern Pennines	4	(1)
Central Pennines	5	(1)
Peak District	1	
Isle of Man	1	(2)
Carneddau	2	(1)
Glyders	1	(1)
Snowdon Group	2	(1)
Moel Hebog Group	1	(1)
Moel Siabod Group	1	(1)
Arennigs	2	(1)
Berwyns	2	(1)
Arans	1	(1)
Rhinogs	1	(1)
Cader Idris Group	2	(1)
Pumlumon	1	(1)
Rhayader Mountains	2	(1)
Radnor Forest	1	
Brecon Beacons	2	
Black Mountains	2	
Dartmoor	1	

Total, 51 days' walking, or 74 days altogether.

NOTES TO TABLE 1

<u>Column 1: Name</u>

The names for mountains as they appear on Ordnance Survey maps are used here throughout, supplemented where necessary by those in common use among mountaineers and hill-walkers. In a very few cases where no official or generally-accepted name could be traced at all, a provisional name has been suggested. Some variation will be noticed in the spelling of Welsh mountain names given both on Ordnance Survey maps and in this book. The orthography of Welsh place-names is at present undergoing revision, and eventually all those which appear to yield a direct and appropriate meaning in the modern language will be spelled in the modern way. Meanwhile, the course adopted here has been to follow the Ordnance Survey spelling except where obviously in error. (See Glossary of Welsh Mountain-names).

<u>Column 2: Height</u>

The heights quoted in feet here are as they appear on one or other of the O.S. maps, supplemented by additional information including details supplied direct by the Ordnance Survey. In a few cases the absence of survey points or stations has enforced reliance on contour rings only, indicated in the Tables by heights followed by a + sign. The altitudes of some summits and several intervening cols may need to be revised whenever the results of new surveys are published. For technical reasons not all O.S. triangulation pillars are situated on exactly the highest points of their respective mountains; owing to the shortage of space on the One-inch Map, it is O.S. policy to print on this map only the <u>station height</u> (which is the altitude at the centre of the base of the pillar) where this height differs from the greatest <u>summit</u> height of the peak. Both values are normally shown on the appropriate Six-inch sheet. The greater height of the two where known is of course the one given in this book.

The metric equivalents of the heights in feet are given here to the nearest metre. Throughout this book the words 'height' and 'altitude' are interchangeable.

<u>Column 3: Maps</u>

The sheet numbers of the maps most useful to mountaineers and hill-walkers are given here. The 1:25000 ($2\frac{1}{2}$") sheet numbers are those of the First Series where appropriate. The Second Series is now making its appearance; it is in double-sheet form, and the sheet numbers are correspondingly double, thus Sheet SX 48/58 covers the same ground as the two First Series sheets numbered SX 48 and 58. An index to the series is printed on the reverse of all 1:25000 sheets. All the sheets of the First Series 1:25000 map have been published for England and Wales but, at the time of writing, the only Second Series sheets depicting two-thousander peaks are those which cover part of the northern fringe of Dartmoor.

Column 4: Grid Reference
A note explaining the system of Grid References is printed at the foot of all medium and small scale O.S. maps. It only remains to add that the figures always identify, by its south-west (bottom left-hand) corner, the square which contains the desired point. The nature of the reference defines the size of the square; thus, a six-figure reference, as used in this book, defines the square of 100-metre sides in which the desired point will be found. A four-figure reference indicates the kilometre square which contains the point, and so on.

Column 6: Position
The details given in this column relate to one or more prominent towns etc. which serve as good centres for visitors. The compass bearing is that from the centre given <u>to</u> the mountain top in each case. Distances are given in miles. Kilometre scales are printed at the foot of all O.S. maps; 1 kilometre = approximately $\frac{5}{8}$th of a mile.

Column 7: Best Ascended From
The compass-bearing given here is that from the mountain top <u>to</u> the nearest point on a road <u>measured in a straight line</u> and ignoring intervening terrain. In few cases will visitors experience difficulties of access, though the property of landowners and farmers should always be respected. Information given in this book should not be taken as evidence of a right of way.

<u>Column 8</u> gives the numbers in their order of altitude as 'separate mountains' and as 'tops', i.e. separate and subsidiary mountains.

<u>Column 9</u> is left open for the reader's use, for a record of the date of his ascent of each peak. A logbook for further details is provided at the end of the tables.

<u>Footnotes</u> printed at the end of each Group in Table 1 give additional details for each top, and sources of information other than the One-inch Map and general usage among mountaineers and hill-walkers. The principal sources include the appropriate sheets of the O.S. 1:25 000 ($2\frac{1}{2}$ inch) and Six-inch Maps, and the following publications:

J.Rooke Corbett, articles in the Rucksack Club Journal, 1911 and 1929

W.T. Elmslie, article in the Fell and Rock Club Journal, 1933

F.H.F.Simpson, article in the Wayfarers' Journal, 1937

E.Moss, article in the Rucksack Club Journal, 1939 and 1940

W.McKnight Docharty, "A Selection of Some 900 British and Irish Mountain
Tops", 1954 and 1962

A. Wainwright, "A Pictorial Guide to the Lakeland Fells" (7 books) 1955-66.
(References to this book are given in the order: book number, chapter,
page number)

For further details of these and other publications see Bibliography.

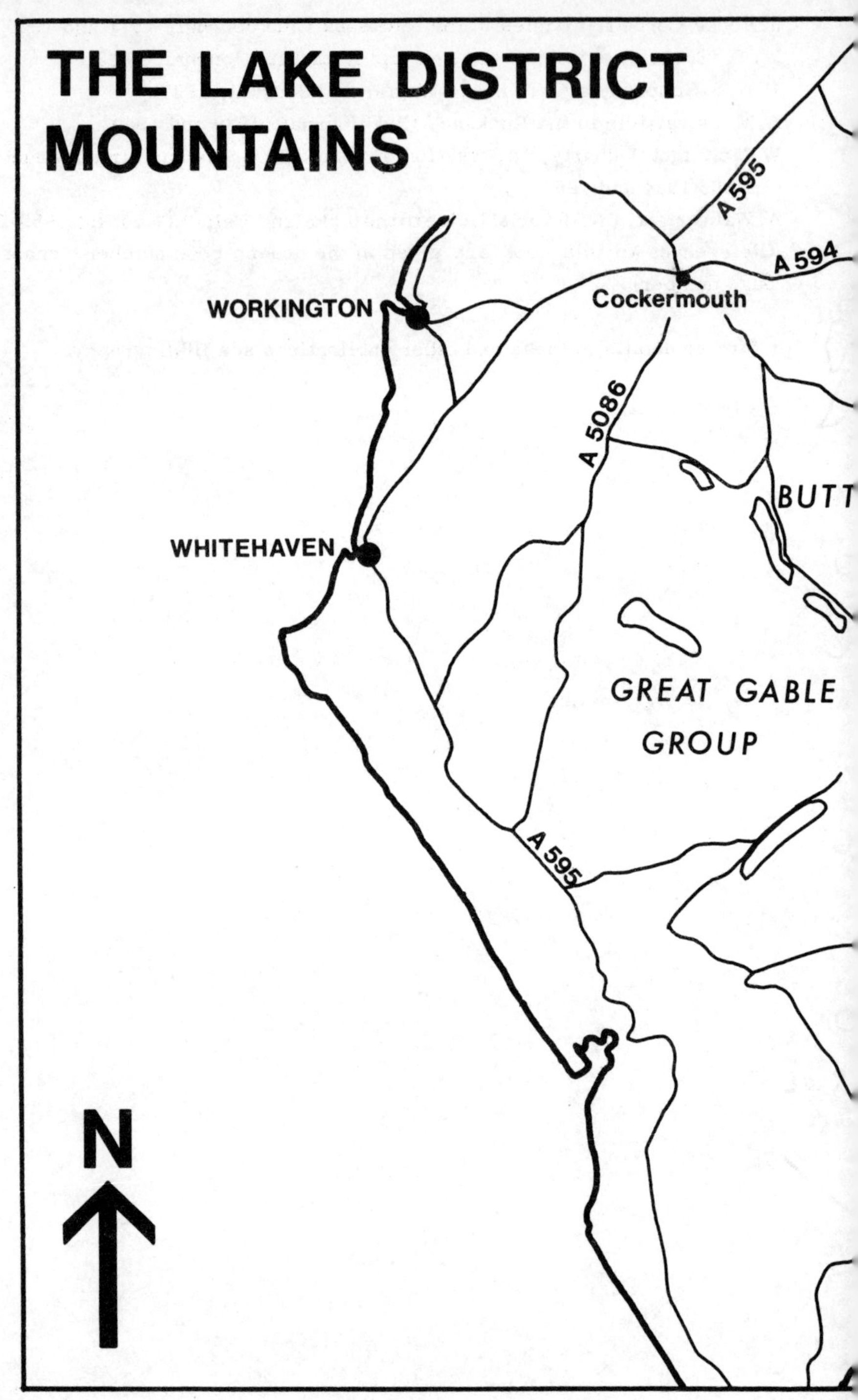

THE LAKE DISTRICT MOUNTAINS
WORKINGTON
Cockermouth
A 595
A 594
A 5086
WHITEHAVEN
BUTT
GREAT GABLE
GROUP
A 595
N

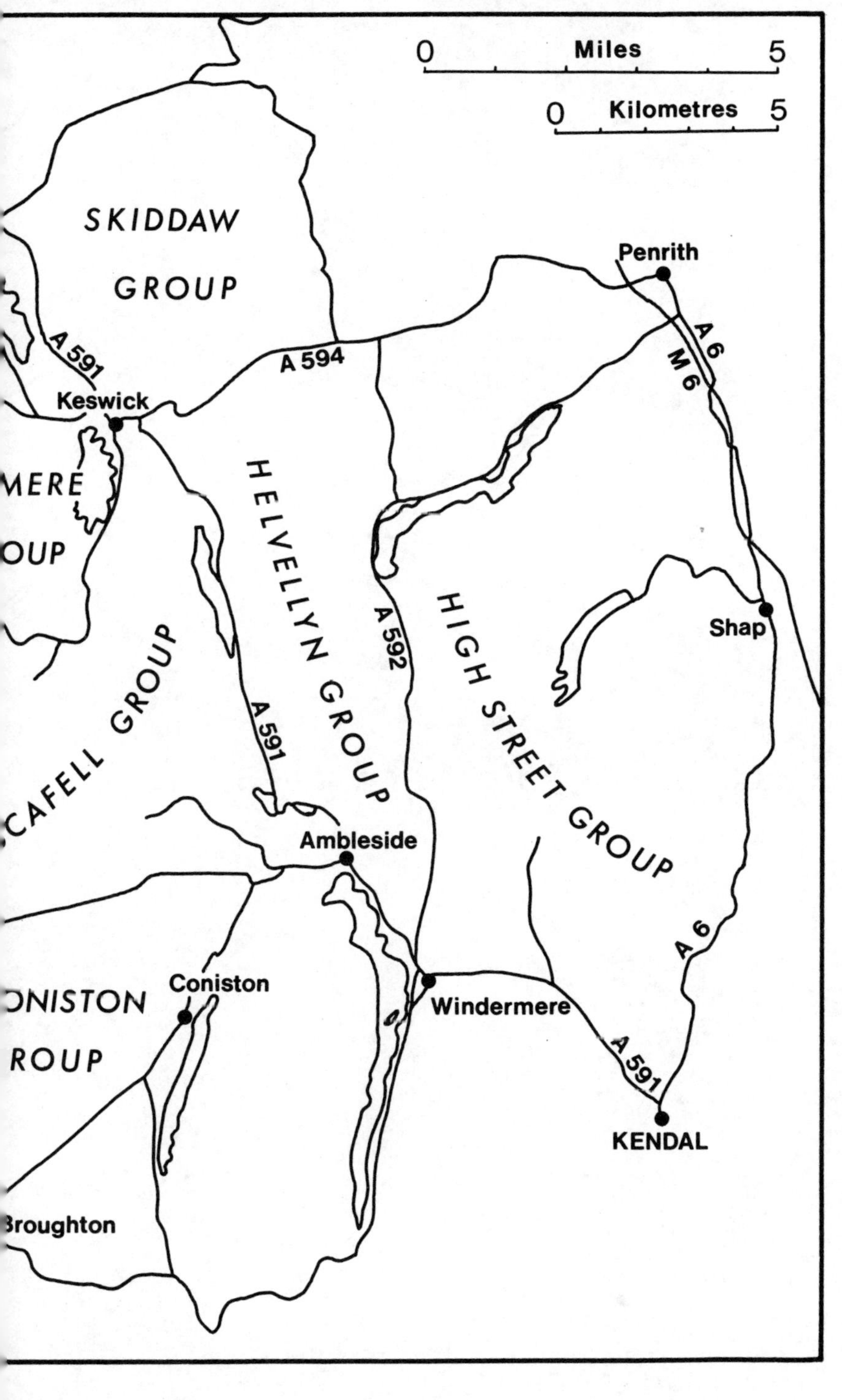

Miles
0   5
Kilometres
0   5
SKIDDAW GROUP
Penrith
A 591
A 594
A 6
M 6
Keswick
MERE
OUP
HELVELLYN GROUP
A 592
HIGH STREET GROUP
Shap
SCAFELL GROUP
A 591
Ambleside
A 6
Coniston
ONISTON
ROUP
Windermere
A 591
KENDAL
Broughton

The mountains of the Lake District - the Cumbrian Mountains, as they should properly be called - rise in a compact group in the extreme north-west corner of England.   The internal arrangement of the district is strikingly wheel-like in plan, especially in the western half of the region where airy mountain ridges alternate with beautiful lake-studded valleys in a unique radiating pattern. To hill-walkers and mountaineers everywhere, the Lake District is sacred ground.   The very names of its highest summits are like a hymn of praise - Great Gable, Pillar, Scafell Pike, Bowfell, Crinkle Crags, Langdale Pikes, The Old Man of Coniston, Fairfield, Helvellyn, High Street, Skiddaw and Blencathra. To most of us, these friendly fells offer a vision of perfection in mountain form against which all other mountains, and all other visions, are measured.   Go where you will, there is nothing better than this.

There are 150 mountains of two thousand feet and over in the Lake District, the greatest concentration of them in England.   Here also are the highest English summits, presided over by Scafell Pike (3210 feet), the highest of all. The principal towns and villages are Keswick, Ambleside, Grasmere, Coniston and Patterdale. Not far away, Kendal, Penrith and Cockermouth perform the function of principal gateways to the district.

Blencathra from Great Gable

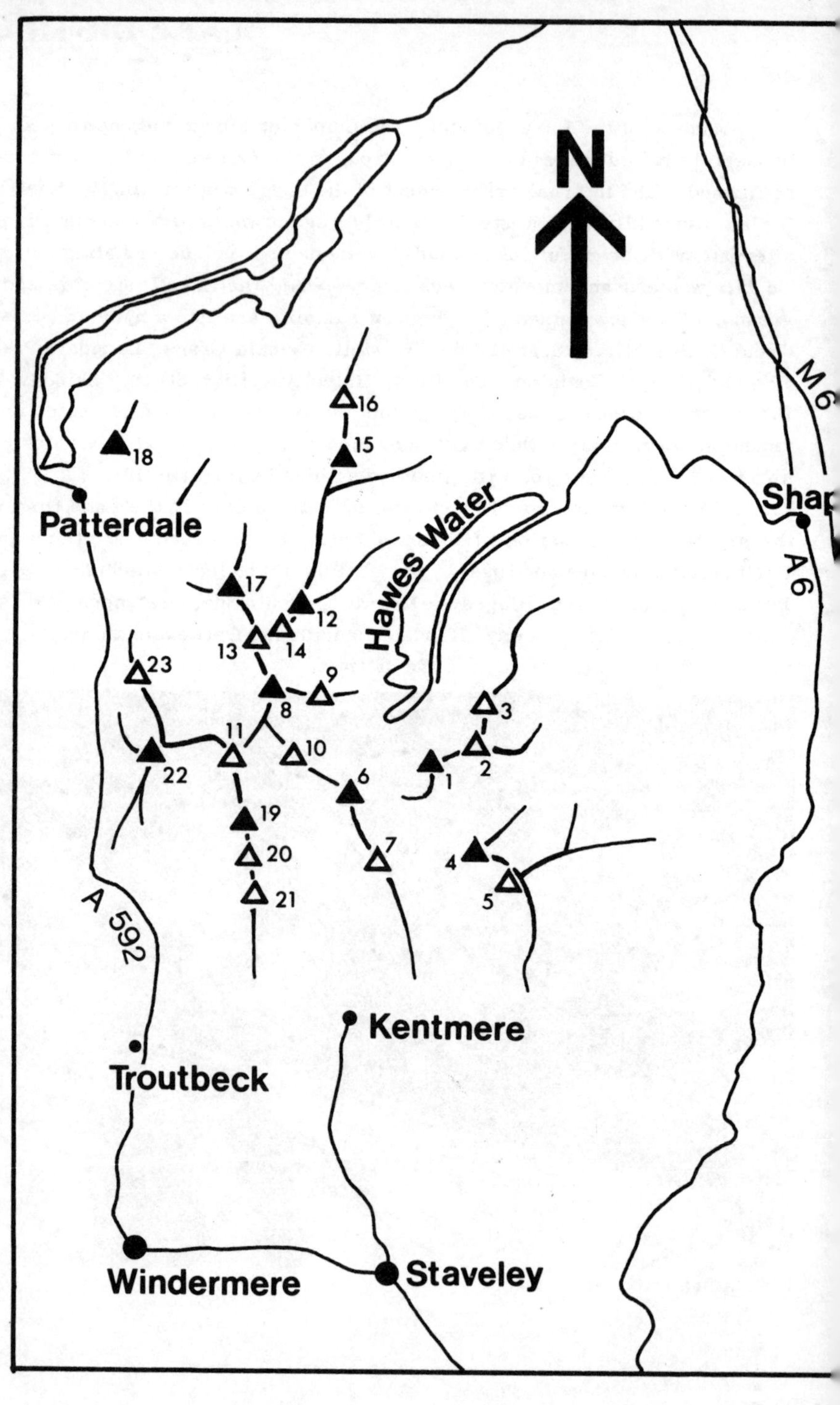

N
M6
Shap
A6
18
16
15
Patterdale
Hawes Water
17
12
13
14
23
9
8
3
11
10
22
1
2
6
19
7
4
20
5
21
A 592
Kentmere
Troutbeck
Windermere
Staveley

▲ **Separate Mountain**

△ **Subsidiary Mountain**

1 Branstree
2 Nowtli Hill
3 Selside Pike
4 Tarn Crag
5 Grey Crag
6 Harter Fell
7 Kentmere Pike
8 High Street
9 Rough Crag
10 Mardale Ill Bell
11 Thornthwaite Crag
12 High Raise
13 The Knott
14 Rampsgill Head
15 Wether Hill
16 Loadpot Hill
17 Rest Dodd
18 Place Fell
19 Ill Bell, Kentmere
20 Froswick
21 Yoke
22 Stony Cove Pike
23 Hartsop Dodd

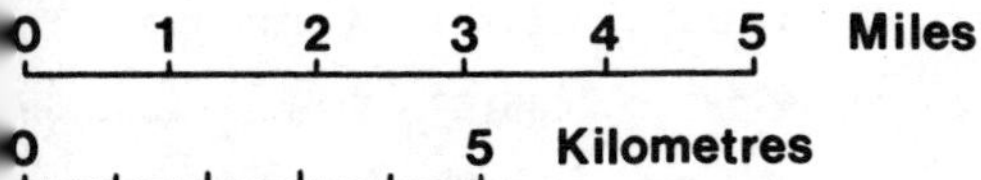

LAKE DISTRICT:
HIGH STREET GROUP

HIGH STREET GROUP

Name	Height feet	metres	Maps 1"	2½"	T	Grid Ref.	County
Branstree[1]	2333	711	83	NY40	T	477099	Westmorland
Nowtli Hill[2]	2209[6]	673	83	NY41	T	487103	Westmorland
Selside Pike	2142	653	83	NY41	T	491111	Westmorland
Tarn Crag	2176	663	83	NY40	T	488077	Westmorland
Grey Crag	2093	638	83	NY40	T	497071	Westmorland
Harter Fell	2539	774	83	NY40	T	460093	Westmorland
Kentmere Pike[3]	2397	731	83	NY40	T	465077	Westmorland
High Street	2719	829	83	NY41	T	440110	Westmorland
Rough Crag	2062	628	83	NY41	T	454112	Westmorland
Mardale Ill Bell	2496[4]	761	83	NY41	T	447101	Westmorland
Thornthwaite Crag[5]	2569	783	83	NY41	T	431099	Westmorland
High Raise	2634	803	83	NY41	T	448134	Westmorland
The Knott	2423	739	83	NY41	T	436126	Westmorland
Rampsgill Head[7]	2581[6]	787	83	NY41	T	443127	Westmorland
Wether Hill[8]	c. 2210[9]	c. 674	83	NY41	T	455167	Westmorland
Loadpot Hill	2202	671	83	NY41	T	456181	Westmorland
Rest Dodd	2278	694	83	NY41	T	432137	Westmorland
Place Fell	2155	657	83	NY41	T	405169	Westmorland
Ill Bell, Kentmere	2476	755	83	NY40	T	436077	Westmorland
Froswick	2359	719	83	NY40	T	435085	Westmorland
Yoke	2309	704	83	NY40	T	437067	Westmorland
Stony Cove Pike[10]	2502	763	83	NY40	T	417099	Westmorland
Hartsop Dodd	2018	615	83	NY41	T	411117	Westmorland

Position	Best Ascended From	No. in order of Altitude		Date Ascended
		Sep. Mtn.	Top	
$\frac{3}{4}$ mi. SSE of Haweswater	Haweswater, $\frac{3}{4}$ mi. to NNW	121	184	
1 mi. SE of Haweswater	Haweswater, 1 mi. to NW	-	252	
1 mi. SE of Haweswater	Haweswater, 1 mi. to NW	-	303	
$2\frac{1}{4}$ mi. SSE of Haweswater	Sadgill, $1\frac{1}{2}$ mi. to SSW	180	276	
$2\frac{3}{4}$ mi. SSE of Haweswater	Sadgill, $1\frac{1}{4}$ mi. to SW	-	327	
1 mi. SSW of Haweswater	Head of Haweswater, 1 mi. to NNE	76	114	
2 mi. S of Haweswater	Brockstones, $1\frac{1}{2}$ mi. to S	-	161	
2 mi. W of Haweswater	Head of Haweswater, $1\frac{3}{4}$ mi. mi. to E	48	68	
1 mi. W of Haweswater	Head of Haweswater, 1 mi. to E	-	339	
$1\frac{1}{2}$ mi. WSW of Haweswater	Head of Haweswater, $1\frac{1}{2}$ mi. to ENE	-	131	
$2\frac{1}{2}$ mi. WSW of Haweswater	Hartsop, $2\frac{1}{2}$ mi. to NW	-	107	
$1\frac{1}{2}$ mi. W of Haweswater	Haweswater, $1\frac{1}{2}$ mi. to E	58	85	
$2\frac{1}{4}$ mi. W of Haweswater	Hartsop, $1\frac{3}{4}$ mi. to W	-	150	
$1\frac{3}{4}$ mi. W of Haweswater	Hartsop, $2\frac{1}{4}$ mi. to W	-	102	
$3\frac{3}{4}$ mi. E of Patterdale	Howtown, 2 mi. to NNW	163	251	
$2\frac{1}{2}$ mi. NW of Haweswater	Howtown, $1\frac{1}{4}$ mi. to NW	-	259	
$2\frac{1}{2}$ mi. SE of Patterdale	Hartsop, $1\frac{1}{2}$ mi. to WSW	140	212	
$\frac{3}{4}$ mi. NE of Patterdale	Patterdale, $\frac{3}{4}$ mi. to SW	187	290	
3 mi. SW of Haweswater	Troutbeck Park, 2 mi. to SW	88	135	
$2\frac{1}{2}$ mi. SW of Haweswater	Troutbeck Park, 2 mi. to SSW	-	174	
$3\frac{3}{4}$ mi. SW of Haweswater	Troutbeck Park, $1\frac{1}{4}$ mi. to SW	-	196	
4 mi. SSE of Patterdale	Kirkstone Pass Inn, $1\frac{1}{2}$ mi. to SW	83	125	
$2\frac{1}{2}$ mi. SSE of Patterdale	Caudale Beck, $\frac{3}{4}$ mi. to WSW	-	379	

<u>Notes</u>

[1] Also: Brant Street (One-inch O.S. map); Artle Crag (Docharty); "Artle Crag W. Top" (Simpson).   A feature called Artlecrag Pike is shown $\frac{1}{4}$ mile to NE on the Six-inch Map.

[2] Author's temporary name, from Nowtli Gill to SE on Six-inch Map. "Mosedale Pike" in Docharty's list, and "Artle Crag E. Top" in Simpson's.

[3] "Raven Crag" (Elmslie).

[4] Six-inch Map: a few yards E of the parish boundary.

[5] "Thornthwaite Beacon" (Docharty).

[6] Six-inch Map.

[7] With a "p" according to Wainwright. (2 Rampsgill Head 1).

[8] Sometimes "Weather Hill".

[9] Wainwright (2 Wether Hill 1).

[10] Also John Bell's Banner, and Caudale Moor.

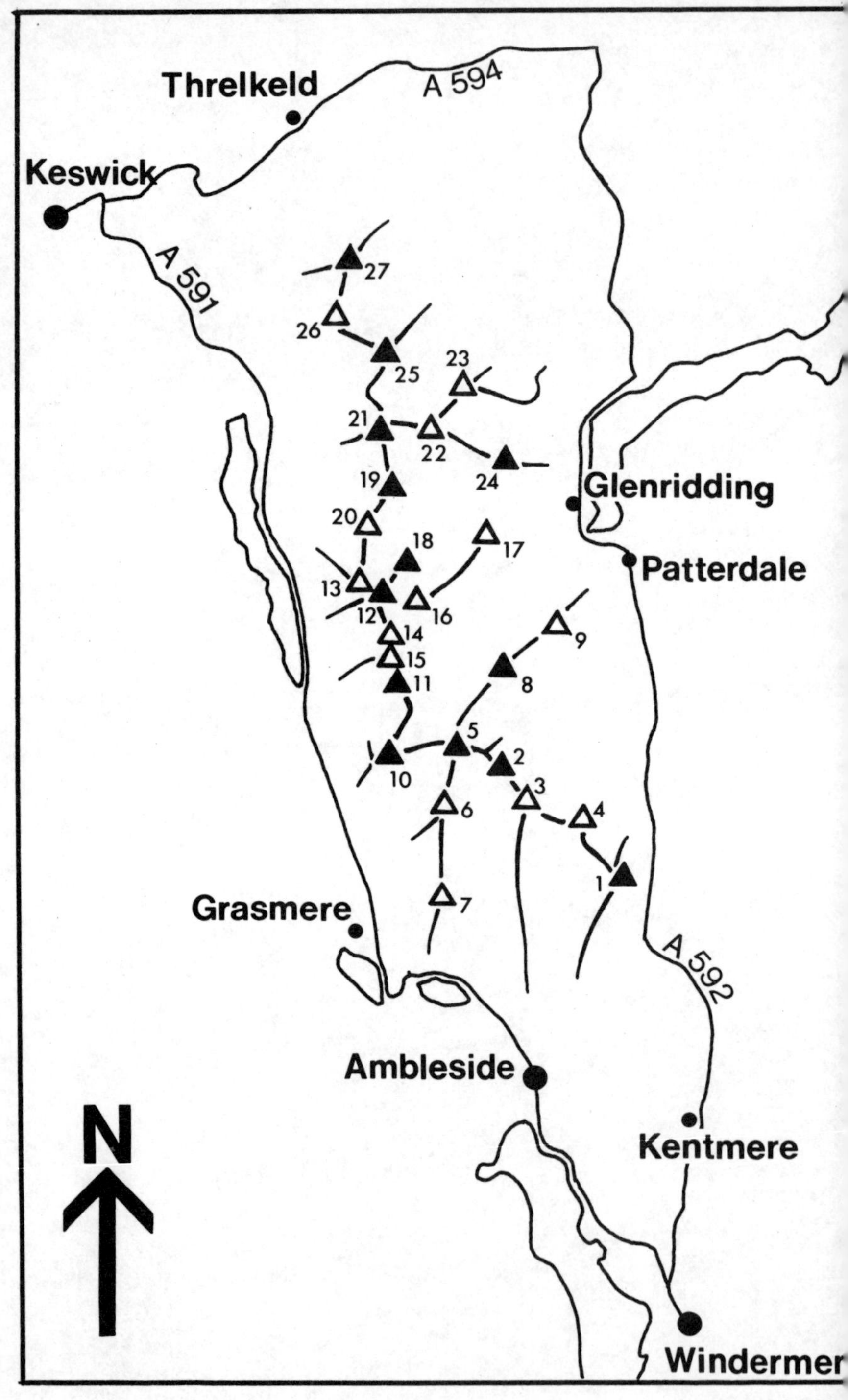

Threlkeld
A 594
Keswick
A 591
27
26
25
23
21
22
24
19
20
18
17
13
12
16
14
15
11
9
8
5
2
3
4
10
6
1
7
Glenridding
Patterdale
Grasmere
A 592
Ambleside
Kentmere
Windermere
N

0   1   2   3   4   5 Miles

0   Kilometres

▲ Separate Mountain

△ Subsidiary Mountain

1 Kilnshaw Chimney
2 Hart Crag
3 Dove Crag
4 Little Hart Crag
5 Fairfield
6 Great Rigg
7 Heron Pike
8 St. Sunday Crag
9 Birks
10 Seat Sandal
11 Dollywaggon Pike
12 Helvellyn
13 Lower Man
14 Nethermost Pike
15 High Crag
16 Striding Edge
17 Birkhouse Moor
18 Catstye Cam
19 Raise
20 White Side
21 Stybarrow Dod
22 Green Side
23 Hart Side
24 Sheffield Pike
25 Great Dodd
26 Calfhow Pike
27 Clough Head

LAKE DISTRICT:

HELVELLYN GROUP

HELVELLYN GROUP

Name	Height feet	metres	Maps 1" 2½" T	Grid Ref.	County
Kilnshaw Chimney [1]	2547	776	83 NY30 T	396087	Westmorland
Hart Crag	2698	822	83 NY31 T	368111	Westmorland
Dove Crag	2603	793	83 NY31 T	374104	Westmorland
Little Hart Crag	2091	637	83 NY31 T	387100	Westmorland
Fairfield	2863	873	83 NY31 T	357117	Westmorland
Great Rigg (<u>summit = Greatrigg Man</u>)	2513	766	83 NY31 T	355103	Westmorland
Heron Pike	2003	611	83 NY30 T	355082	Westmorland
St. Sunday Crag (<u>summit = The Cape</u>[6])	2756	840	83 NY31 T	369133	Westmorland
Birks	2040	622	83 NY31 T	381144	Westmorland
Seat Sandal	2415	736	83 NY31 T	343115	Westmorland
Dollywaggon Pike	2810	856	83 NY31 T	345130	Cumberland and Westmorland
Helvellyn [2]	3116[3]	949	83 NY31 T	341151	Cumberland and Westmorland
Lower Man	3033	924	83 NY31 T	337155	Cumberland and Westmorland
Nethermost Pike	2920[6]	890	83 NY31 T	343141	Cumberland and Westmorland
High Crag	2896[6]	883	83 NY31 T	342137	Cumberland and Westmorland
Striding Edge (<u>summit = High Spying How</u>[6])	2832[6]	863	83 NY31 T	349149	Westmorland
Birkhouse Moor	2353[6]	717	83 NY31 T	363159	Westmorland
Catstye Cam [4]	2917	889	83 NY31 T	348158	Westmorland
Raise	2889	881	83 NY31 T	343174	Cumberland and Westmorland
White Side (<u>summit = Whiteside Bank</u>[6])	2832	863	83 NY31 T	337166	Cumberland and Westmorland
Stybarrow Dod	c. 2770[5]	c. 844	83 NY31 T	343189	Cumberland and Westmorland

Position	Best Ascended From	No. in order of Altitude		Date Asc-ended
		Sep. Mtn.	Top	
$4\frac{1}{4}$ mi. S of Patterdale	Kirkstone Pass Inn, $\frac{1}{2}$ mi. to SSE	75	113	
$3\frac{1}{4}$ mi. SSW of Patterdale	Rydal, 3 mi. to S	51	74	
$3\frac{1}{2}$ mi. SSW of Patterdale	Rydal, $2\frac{1}{2}$ mi. to S	-	97	
$3\frac{1}{2}$ mi. S of Patterdale	Kirkstone Pass Inn, $1\frac{1}{2}$ mi. to SE	-	328	
$3\frac{1}{2}$ mi. SW of Patterdale	Grasmere, 3 mi. to SSE; Rydal, $3\frac{1}{4}$ mi. to S	32	40	
$4\frac{1}{4}$ mi. SW of Patterdale	Rydal, $2\frac{1}{2}$ mi. to S	-	122	
3 mi. NNW of Ambleside	Rydal, $1\frac{1}{4}$ mi. to S	-	390	
$2\frac{1}{4}$ mi. SW of Patterdale	Patterdale, $2\frac{1}{4}$ mi. to NE	44	59	
$1\frac{1}{4}$ mi. SW of Patterdale	Patterdale, $1\frac{1}{4}$ mi. to NE	-	355	
$2\frac{1}{2}$ mi. N of Grasmere	Grasmere, $2\frac{1}{2}$ mi. to S	102	154	
$3\frac{1}{2}$ mi. SW of Patterdale	Dunmail Raise, $1\frac{1}{2}$ mi. to SW	36	49	
$3\frac{1}{2}$ mi. W of Patterdale	Thirlspot, 2 mi. to NW; Dunmail Raise, $2\frac{1}{4}$ mi. to SSW; Patterdale, $3\frac{1}{2}$ mi. to E	12	12	
$3\frac{1}{2}$ mi. W of Patterdale	Thirlspot, $1\frac{3}{4}$ mi. to NW	-	17	
$3\frac{1}{2}$ mi. WSW of Patterdale	Dunmail Raise, $1\frac{3}{4}$ mi. to SW	-	32	
$3\frac{1}{2}$ mi. WSW of Patterdale	Dunmail Raise, $1\frac{3}{4}$ mi. to SW	-	37	
3 mi. W of Patterdale	Patterdale, 3 mi. to E	-	45	
2 mi. W of Patterdale	Patterdale, 2 mi. to E	-	176	
3 mi. W of Patterdale	Patterdale, 3 mi. to E	27	33	
$3\frac{1}{4}$ mi. WNW of Patterdale	Thirlspot, $1\frac{1}{2}$ mi. to WNW	31	38	
$3\frac{1}{2}$ mi. WNW of Patterdale	Thirlspot, $1\frac{1}{2}$ mi. to NW	-	46	
$3\frac{3}{4}$ mi. WNW of Patterdale	Stanah, $1\frac{1}{2}$ mi. to W	42	56	

Green Side (summit = White Stones)	2600	792	83 NY31 T	353187	Cumberland and Westmorland
Hart Side	2481	756	83 NY31 T	358197	Cumberland
Sheffield Pike	2232	680	83 NY31 T	369181	Westmorland
Great Dodd	2807	856	83 NY32 T	342204	Cumberland
Calfhow Pike	2166	660	83 NY32 T	330211	Cumberland
Clough Head[7]	2381	726	83 NY32 T	333225	Cumberland

<u>Notes</u>

[1] Also: Red Screes.

[2] Westmorland County Top.

[3] O.S. letter of 1971 November 2. The altitude 3113 given on the 1970 O.S. One-inch Tourist Map is that at the base of the triangulation pillar near the summit.

[4] Also known as Catstycam, and Catchedicam.

[5] Wainwright. (1 Stybarrow Dod 7). Point 2756 (One-inch Map) is at Grid Reference 340186.

[6] Six-inch Map.

[7] Also: White Pike.

3 mi. NW of Patterdale	Glenridding, $2\frac{1}{4}$ mi. to ESE	-	99
$3\frac{1}{2}$ mi. NW of Patterdale	Glencoyne Bridge, $1\frac{3}{4}$ mi. to ESE	-	133
$1\frac{1}{4}$ mi. NW of Glenridding	Glenridding, $1\frac{1}{4}$ mi. to SE	153	236
$4\frac{1}{2}$ mi. NW of Patterdale	Stanah, $1\frac{3}{4}$ mi. to SW	37	50
5 mi. NW of Patterdale	Old Coach Road, $1\frac{1}{2}$ mi. to NE	-	283
$5\frac{1}{2}$ mi. NNW of Patterdale	Old Coach Road, $\frac{3}{4}$ mi. to N	108	165

Striding Edge and Helvellyn

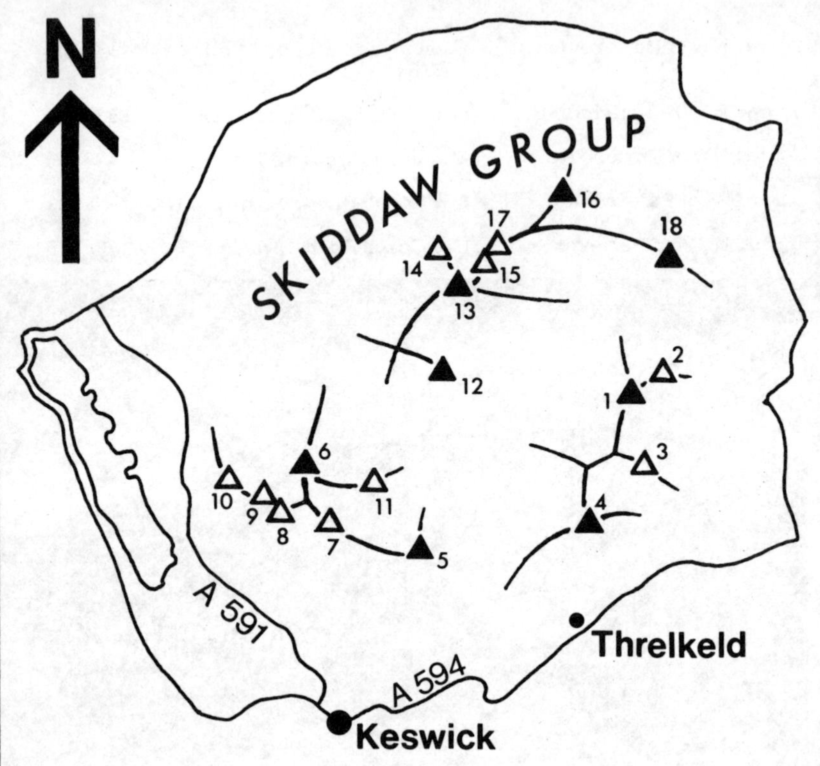

1	Bowscale Fell	10	Ullock Pike
2	Tarn Crags Top	11	Sale How
3	Bannerdale Crags	12	Great Calva
4	Blencathra	13	Knott
5	Lonscale Fell	14	Great Sca Fell
6	Skiddaw	15	Miller Moss
7	Little Man	16	High Pike
8	Carl Side	17	Great Lingy Hill
9	Long Side	18	Carrock Fell

LAKE DISTRICT:

SKIDDAW GROUP

CONISTON GROUP

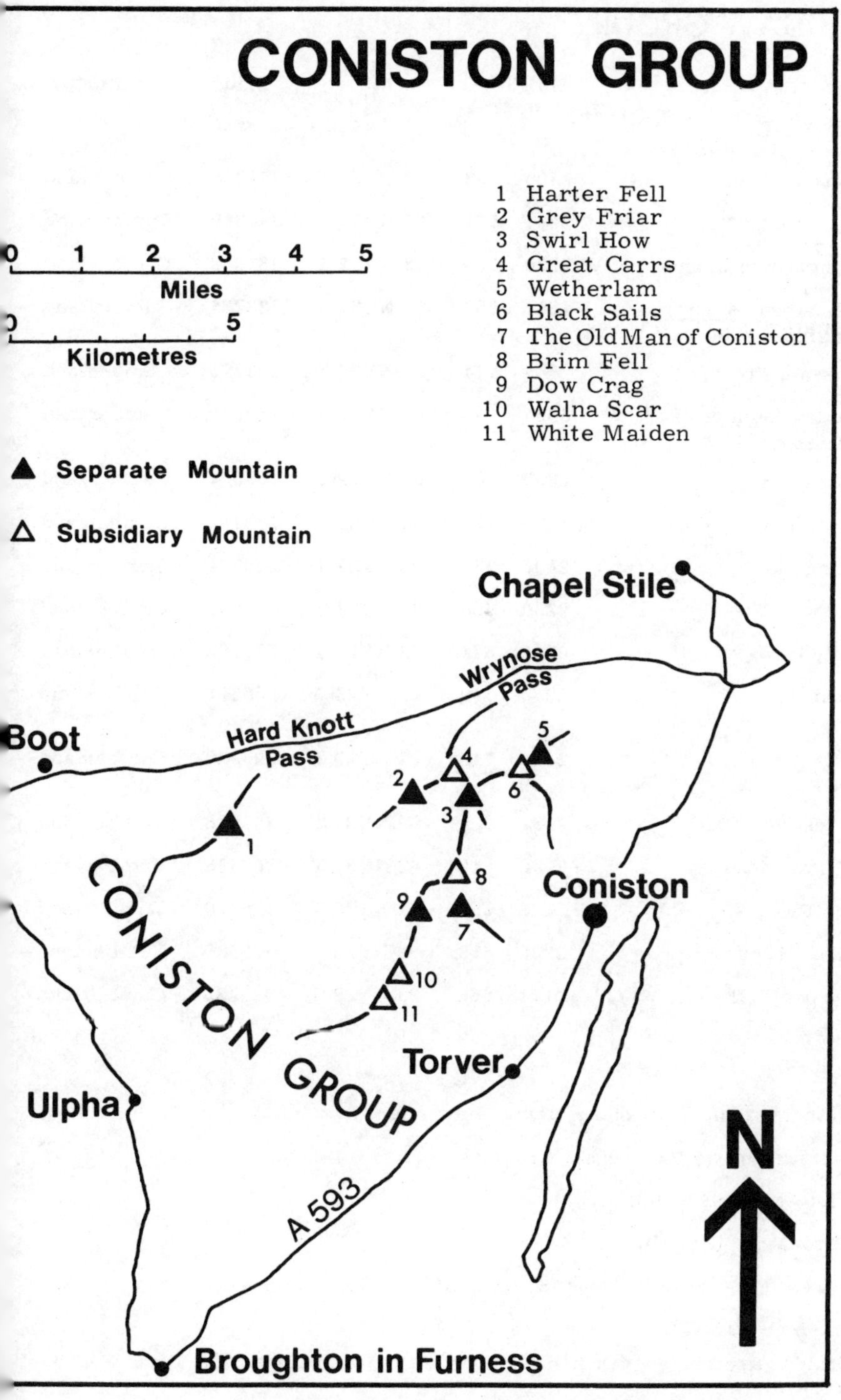

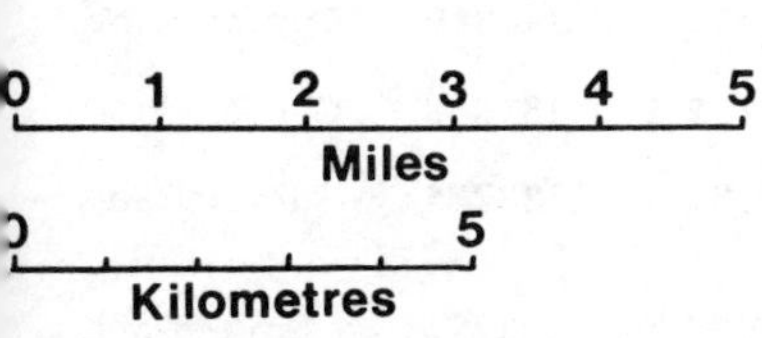

SKIDDAW GROUP

Name	Height feet	metres	Maps 1" 2½" T	Grid Ref.	County
Bowscale Fell	2306	703	83 NY33 T	333305	Cumberland
Tarn Crags Top [1]	2200+	671+	83 NY33 T	340310	Cumberland
Bannerdale Crags	c. 2230 [2]	c. 680	83 NY32 T	336289	Cumberland
Blencathra [3] (summit = Hallsfell Top)	2847	868	82 NY32 T	323277	Cumberland
Lonscale Fell	'2344	714	82 NY22 T	285271	Cumberland
Skiddaw (summit = Skiddaw Man [6])	3054	931	82 NY22 T	260290	Cumberland
Little Man [4]	2837	865	82 NY22 T	266277	Cumberland
Carl Side	c. 2420 [2]	c. 738	82 NY22 T	254281	Cumberland
Long Side	2405	733	82 NY22 T	248284	Cumberland
Ullock Pike	2230	680	82 NY22 T	243288	Cumberland
Sale How	2200+	671+	82 NY22 T	276286	Cumberland
Great Calva	2265	690	82 NY23 T	290311	Cumberland
Knott	2329	710	82 NY23 T	296329	Cumberland
Great Sca Fell [5]	2131 [7]	650	82 NY23 T	291338	Cumberland
Miller Moss	2000 [6]	610	82 NY33 T	303338	Cumberland
High Pike	2159	658	82 NY33 T	318350	Cumberland
Great Lingy Hill	2009 [6]	612	82 NY33 T	309339	Cumberland
Carrock Fell	2174	663	83 NY33 T	341336	Cumberland

Notes

[1] Author's temporary name, from feature to NW.

[2] Wainwright. (5 Bannerdale Crags 1)

[3] Also known as Saddleback.

[4] "Low Man" (Elmslie).

[5] "Great Lingy Hill E. Top" (Simpson).

[6] Six-inch Map.

[7] Could be a little higher than this, according to Wainwright (5 Great Sca Fell 8).

42

Position	Best Ascended From	No. in order of Altitude		Date Asc-ended
		Sep. Mtn.	Top	
6 mi. NE of Keswick	Mungrisdale, 2 mi. to E	132	198	
6½ mi. NE of Keswick	Mungrisdale, 1½ mi. to ESE	-	263	
5½ mi. NE of Keswick	Scales, 1½ mi. to SSE	-	238	
4½ mi. NE of Keswick	Threlkeld, 1½ mi. to S	34	42	
2½ mi. NNE of Keswick	Keswick, 2½ mi. to SSW	117	178	
3½ mi. N of Keswick	Keswick, 3½ mi. to S	15	16	
2½ mi. N of Keswick	Keswick, 2½ mi. to S	-	44	
3 mi. NNW of Keswick	Keswick, 3 mi. to SSE	-	151	
3¼ mi. NNW of Keswick	Keswick, 3¼ mi. to SSE	-	158	
3½ mi. NNW of Keswick	Ravenstone, ¾ mi. to NW	-	240	
3¼ mi. N of Keswick	Keswick, 3¼ mi. to S	-	262	
5 mi. NNE of Keswick	Unclassified road, 2½ mi. to WNW	145	219	
6 mi. NNE of Keswick	Unclassified road, 2½ mi. to W	124	187	
6½ mi. NNE of Keswick	Longlands, 2 mi. to NW	-	308	
7 mi. NNE of Keswick	Fell Side, 2¼ mi. to N	-	408	
8 mi. NNE of Keswick	Fell Side, 1¾ mi. to NNW	186	287	
7 mi. NNE of Keswick	Fell Side, 2¼ mi. to N	-	386	
7¾ mi. NE of Keswick	Mosedale, 1¼ mi. to SE	182	278	

<table>
<tr><td>

BUTTERMERE GROUP

1 High Spy
2 Dale Head
3 Hindscarth
4 Robinson
5 Crag Hill
6 Wanlope
7 Whiteless Pike
8 Sail
9 Scar Crags
10 Causey Pike
11 Grasmoor
12 Grisedale Pike
13 Hopegill Head
14 Ladyside Pike
15 Whiteside

</td><td>

GREAT GABLE GROUP

1 Great Gable
2 Green Gable
3 Base Brown
4 Kirk Fell West
5 Kirk Fell East
6 Pillar Fell
7 Pillar Rock
8 Looking Stead
9 Little Scoat Fell
10 Middle Scoat Fell
11 Great Scoat Fell
12 Steeple
13 Red Pike (Wasdale)
14 Yewbarrow
15 Stirrup Crag
16 Haycock
17 Caw Fell
18 Seatallan
19 Iron Crag
20 Brandreth
21 Grey Knotts
22 Fleetwith Pike
23 High Crag
24 High Stile
25 Red Pike (Ennerdale)
26 Starling Dodd
27 Great Borne

</td></tr>
</table>

Miles 0 ————— 5

Kilometres 0 ————— 5

LAKE DISTRICT:
BUTTERMERE GROUP
GREAT GABLE GROUP

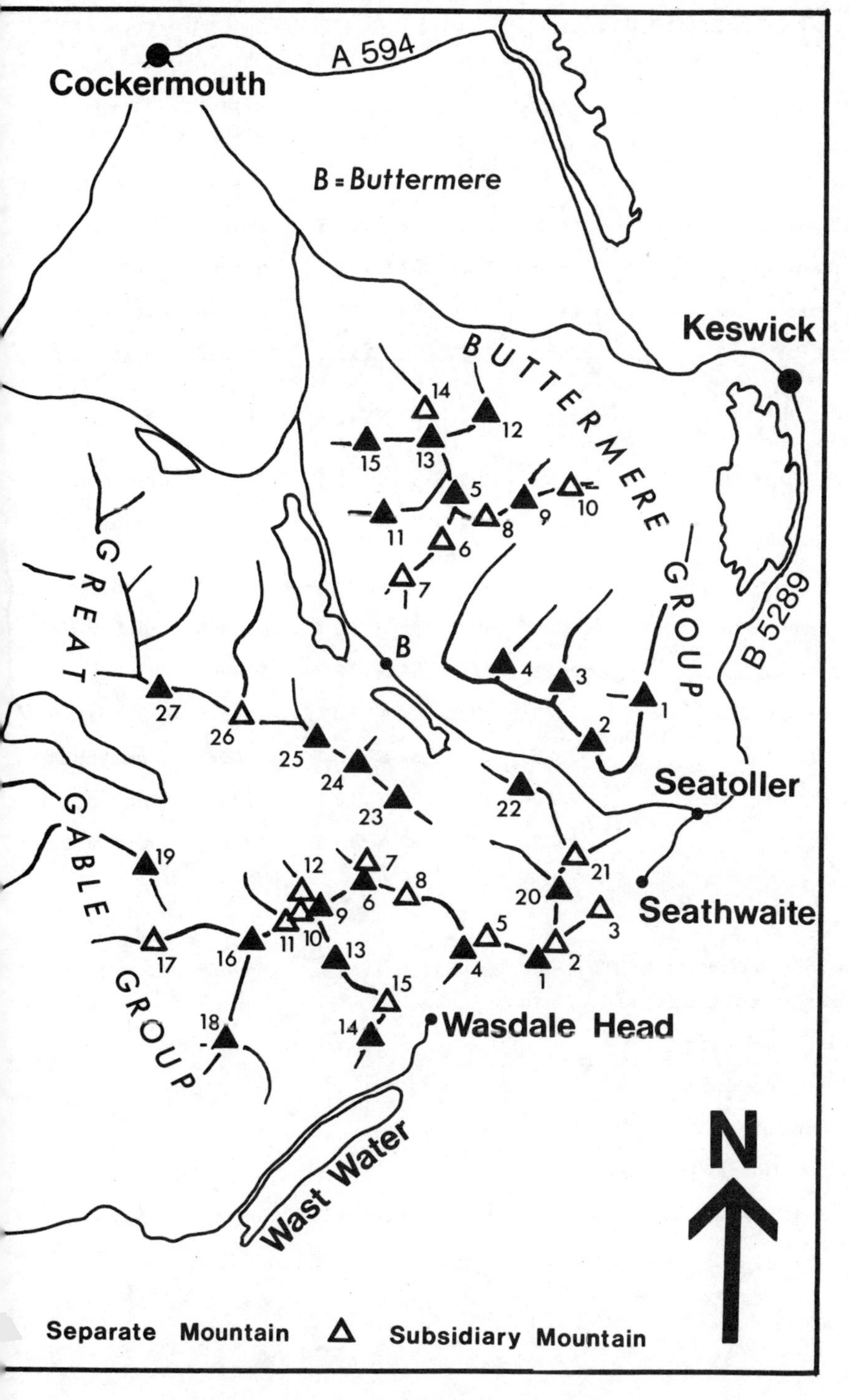

Cockermouth
A 594
B = Buttermere
Keswick
BUTTERMERE GROUP
B 5289
GREAT
GABLE
GROUP
B
Seatoller
Seathwaite
Wasdale Head
West Water
N
Separate Mountain   Subsidiary Mountain

BUTTERMERE GROUP

Name	Height feet	metres	Maps 1" 2½" T	Grid Ref.	County
High Spy [1]	2143	653	82 NY21 T	234162	Cumberland
Dale Head	2473	754	82 NY21 T	223153	Cumberland
Hindscarth	2385	727	82 NY21 T	215165	Cumberland
Robinson	2417	737	82 NY21 T	201168	Cumberland
Crag Hill [2]	2753	839	82 NY12 T	192203	Cumberland
Wanlope [3]	2533	772	82 NY11 T	188197	Cumberland
Whiteless Pike	2159	658	82 NY11 T	180189	Cumberland
Sail	c. 2530 [4]	c. 771	82 NY12 T	198202	Cumberland
Scar Crags	2205	672	82 NY22 T	209206	Cumberland
Causey Pike	c. 2035 [4]	c. 620	82 NY22 T	217209	Cumberland
Grasmoor	2791	851	82 NY12 T	174203	Cumberland
Grisedale Pike	2593	790	82 NY12 T	198225	Cumberland
Hopegill Head [5]	2525	770	82 NY12 T	185221	Cumberland
Ladyside Pike [7]	2300+	701+	82 NY12 T	184227	Cumberland
Whiteside	2317	706	82 NY12 T	170219	Cumberland

Notes

[1] Also: Scawdel Fell (Bartholomew's Half-inch and One-inch Maps); also known as Eel Crags, and Lobstone Band.

[2] Also: Eel Crag.

[3] Also: Wandope.

[4] According to Wainwright (6 Sail 1).

[5] Also: Hobcarton Pike.

[7] Also previously known as Lady's Seat, according to Wainwright. (6 Hopegill Head 6).

<table>
<tr><td></td><td></td><td colspan="2">No. in
order of
Altitude</td><td>Date
Asc-
ended</td></tr>
<tr><td>Position</td><td>Best Ascended From</td><td>Sep.
Mtn.</td><td>Top</td><td></td></tr>
<tr><td>3½ mi. E of Buttermere</td><td>Grange, 1¼ mi. to NE</td><td>194</td><td>302</td><td></td></tr>
<tr><td>3 mi. ESE of Buttermere</td><td>Honister Pass, 1 mi. to S</td><td>90</td><td>137</td><td></td></tr>
<tr><td>2½ mi. E of Buttermere</td><td>Honister Pass, 2 mi. to SSE</td><td>106</td><td>162</td><td></td></tr>
<tr><td>1½ mi. E of Buttermere</td><td>Hassness, 1 mi. to SW</td><td>101</td><td>153</td><td></td></tr>
<tr><td>2¼ mi. NNE of Buttermere</td><td>Buttermere village, 2¼ mi. to SSW</td><td>45</td><td>60</td><td></td></tr>
<tr><td>1¾ mi. NNE of Buttermere</td><td>Buttermere village, 1¾ mi. to SSW</td><td>-</td><td>116</td><td></td></tr>
<tr><td>1¼ mi. N of Buttermere</td><td>Buttermere village 1¼ mi. to S</td><td>-</td><td>288</td><td></td></tr>
<tr><td>2½ mi. NE of Buttermere</td><td>Buttermere village, 2½ mi. to SW</td><td>-</td><td>117</td><td></td></tr>
<tr><td>3 mi. NE of Buttermere</td><td>Stoneycroft, 1¾ mi. to E</td><td>167</td><td>256</td><td></td></tr>
<tr><td>3½ mi. NE of Buttermere</td><td>Stoneycroft, 1¼ mi. to E</td><td>-</td><td>362</td><td></td></tr>
<tr><td>2 mi. N of Buttermere</td><td>Buttermere village, 2 mi. to S</td><td>40</td><td>53</td><td></td></tr>
<tr><td>3¾ mi. NNE of Buttermere</td><td>Braithwaite, 2 mi. to NE</td><td>67</td><td>100</td><td></td></tr>
<tr><td>3¼ mi. N of Buttermere</td><td>Hopebeck, 1½ mi. to NW</td><td>80</td><td>120</td><td></td></tr>
<tr><td>3½ mi. N of Buttermere</td><td>Hopebeck, 1½ mi. to NW</td><td>-</td><td>203</td><td></td></tr>
<tr><td>3 mi. N of Buttermere</td><td>Brackenthwaite, 1 mi. to W</td><td>129</td><td>194</td><td></td></tr>
</table>

GREAT GABLE GROUP

Name	Height		Maps	Grid	County
	feet	metres	1" 2½" T	Ref.	
Great Gable	2949	899	82 NY21 T	210102	Cumberland
Green Gable	2603	793	82 NY21 T	214106	Cumberland
Base Brown	2120	646	82 NY21 T	225114	Cumberland
Kirk Fell West	2630	802	82 NY11 T	194104	Cumberland
Kirk Fell East	2579[6]	786	82 NY11 T	199107	Cumberland
Pillar Fell	2928	892	82 NY11 T	171120	Cumberland
Pillar Rock	2500+[1]	762+	82 NY11 T	171123	Cumberland
Looking Stead	2058	627	82 NY11 T	186117	Cumberland
Little Scoat Fell[2]	2760	841	82 NY11 T	159113	Cumberland
Middle Scoat Fell[2]	2750+	838+	82 NY11 T	157113	Cumberland
Great Scoat Fell[2]	2750+	838+	82 NY11 T	153111	Cumberland
Steeple	2687	819	82 NY11 T	157116	Cumberland
Red Pike (in Wasdale)	2707[6]	825	82 NY11 T	165106	Cumberland
Yewbarrow	2058	627	82 NY10 T	173084	Cumberland
Stirrup Crag[3]	2009	612	82 NY10 T	175092	Cumberland
Haycock	2618	798	82 NY11 T	144107	Cumberland
Caw Fell	2288	697	82 NY11 T	131109	Cumberland
Seatallan	2270	692	82 NY10 T	139084	Cumberland
Iron Crag	2100+	640+	82 NY11 T	122119	Cumberland
Brandreth	2344	714	82 NY21 T	214119	Cumberland
Grey Knotts	2287	697	82 NY21 T	219126	Cumberland
Fleetwith Pike	2126	648	82 NY21 T	206141	Cumberland
High Crag	2443	745	82 NY11 T	180140	Cumberland
High Stile	2644	806	82 NY11 T	169147	Cumberland
Red Pike (in Ennerdale)	2479	756	82 NY11 T	160154	Cumberland

		No. in order of Altitude		Date Asc- ended
Position	Best Ascended From	Sep. Mtn.	Top	
3 mi. SW of Seatoller	Wasdale Head, $1\frac{3}{4}$ mi. to WSW; Seathwaite, $1\frac{3}{4}$ mi. to ENE	22	27	
$2\frac{3}{4}$ mi. SW of Seatoller	Seathwaite, $1\frac{1}{2}$ mi. to ENE	-	98	
2 mi. SW of Seatoller	Seathwaite, $\frac{3}{4}$ mi. to ENE	-	313	
$3\frac{3}{4}$ mi. SW of Seatoller	Wasdale Head, $1\frac{1}{4}$ mi. to SSW	61	88	
$3\frac{1}{2}$ mi. SW of Seatoller	Wasdale Head, $1\frac{1}{2}$ mi. to SSW	-	103	
$4\frac{3}{4}$ mi. WSW of Seatoller	Gillerthwaite, 2 mi. to NW; Wasdale Head, $2\frac{1}{4}$ mi. to SSE	25	30	
$4\frac{3}{4}$ mi. W of Seatoller	Gillerthwaite, 2 mi. to NW; Wasdale Head, $2\frac{1}{2}$ mi. to SSE	-	127	
$3\frac{3}{4}$ mi. WSW of Seatoller	Wasdale Head, $1\frac{3}{4}$ mi. to S	-	343	
$5\frac{1}{2}$ mi. WSW of Seatoller	Gillerthwaite, 2 mi. to NW	43	58	
$5\frac{3}{4}$ mi. WSW of Seatoller	Gillerthwaite, 2 mi. to NW	-	63	
6 mi. WSW of Seatoller	Gillerthwaite, 2 mi. to NNW	-	61	
$5\frac{1}{2}$ mi. WSW of Seatoller	Gillerthwaite, 2 mi. to NNW	-	76	
$5\frac{1}{4}$ mi. WSW of Seatoller	Bowderdale, 2 mi. to S	50	71	
$5\frac{1}{2}$ mi. SW of Seatoller	Bowderdale, 1 mi. SSW	217	344	
5 mi. SW of Seatoller	Bowderdale, $1\frac{1}{2}$ mi. to SSW	-	387	
$6\frac{1}{2}$ mi. WSW of Seatoller	Wast Water, $2\frac{3}{4}$ mi. to SE	64	92	
$7\frac{1}{4}$ mi. WSW of Seatoller	Gillerthwaite, 2 mi. to NNE	-	207	
$7\frac{1}{4}$ mi. SW of Seatoller	Buckbarrow, 2 mi. to S	142	216	
$7\frac{3}{4}$ mi. W of Seatoller	Gillerthwaite, $1\frac{1}{2}$ mi. to NE	203	321	
$2\frac{1}{4}$ mi. SW of Seatoller	Seathwaite, $1\frac{1}{4}$ mi. to E	116	177	
$1\frac{3}{4}$ mi. WSW of Seatoller	Seathwaite, 1 mi. to ESE	-	209	
$2\frac{1}{4}$ mi. W of Seatoller	Gatesgarth, $\frac{3}{4}$ mi. to NW	197	310	
4 mi. W of Seatoller	Gatesgarth, 1 mi. to NE	98	146	
$4\frac{3}{4}$ mi. W of Seatoller	Gatesgarth, $1\frac{1}{2}$ mi. to E	56	83	
$5\frac{1}{4}$ mi. W of Seatoller	Buttermere village, $1\frac{1}{4}$ mi. to NE	87	134	

| Starling Dodd | 2085 | 636 | 82 NY11 T | 142157 | Cumberland |
| Great Borne[4] | 2020 | 616 | 82 NY11 T | 123163 | |

<u>Notes</u>

[1] According to Simpson.

[2] According to the $2\frac{1}{2}$" Map contours.

[3] "Yewbarrow N. Top" (Simpson).

[4] Also known as Herdus = Herdhouse (Wainwright 7 Great Borne 2).

[6] Six-inch Map.

<u>Warning Note</u>

Pillar Rock is the only mountain in England and Wales whose summit is not readily accessible to the mountain walker who is not also a rock-climber. The easiest way to the top is something between a very exposed scramble and an easy rock-climb. Non-rock-climbers would be well advised to ask one of their climbing friends to take them up it.
(For further reference see the topographical account, and the plan of the Rock and its surroundings, in the climbers' guidebook <u>Pillar Rock</u> published by the Fell and Rock Climbing Club).

| 6½ mi. W of Seatoller | Buttermere village, 2¼ mi to ENE | - | 330 |
| 7¾ mi. WNW of Seatoller | Anglers' Hotel, 1½ mi. to W | 233 | 378 |

Pillar Fell from the Wastwater Hotel

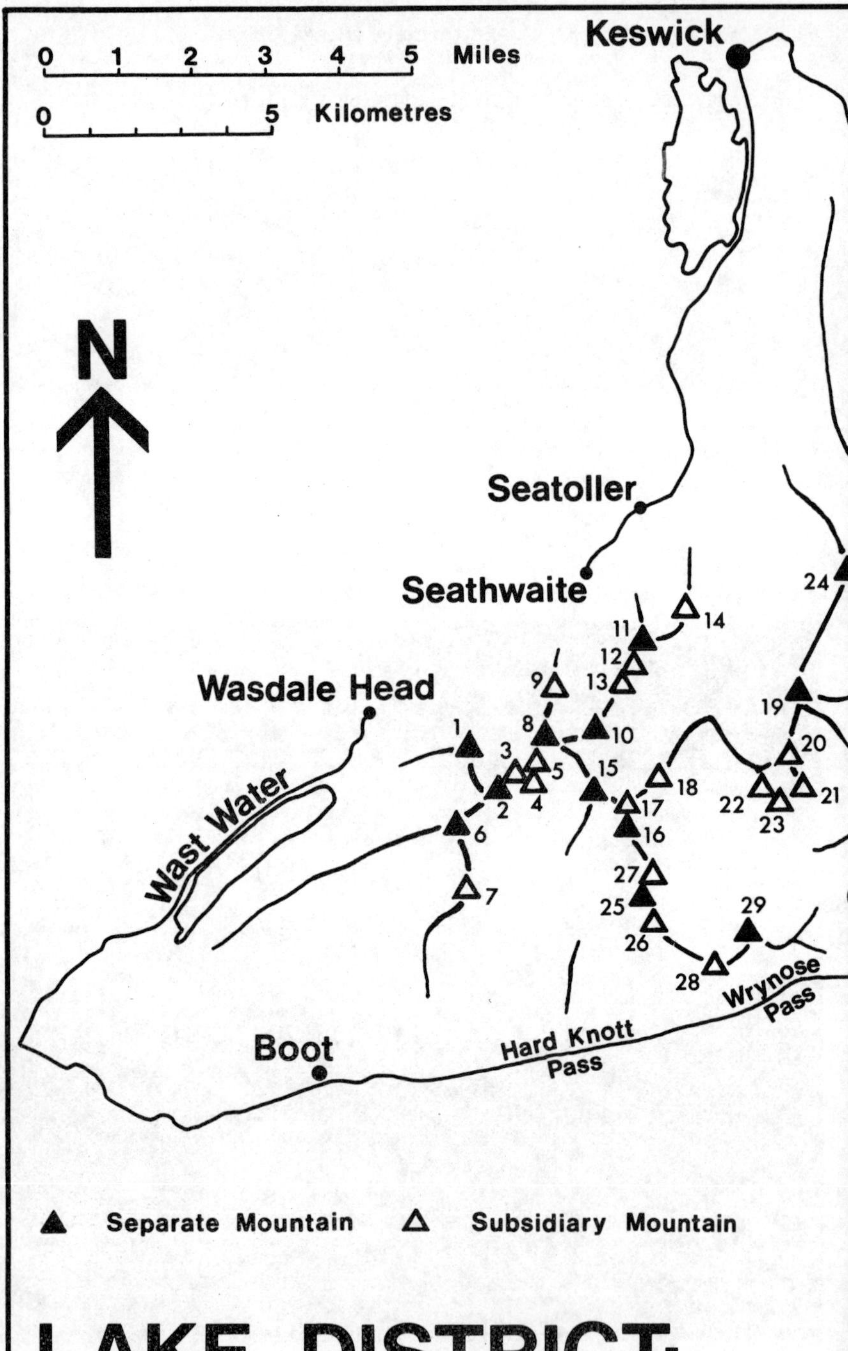

LAKE DISTRICT:

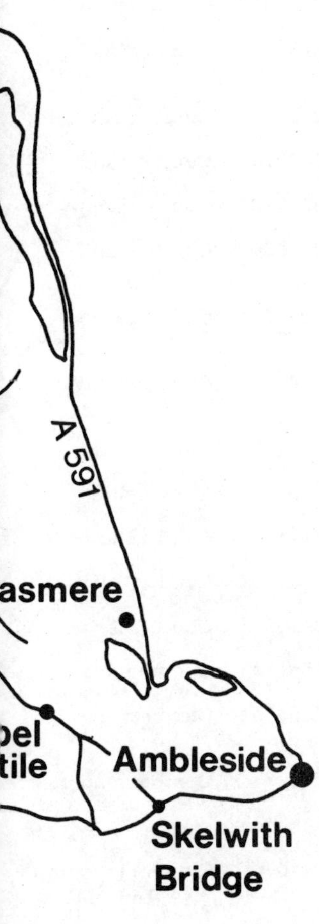

1 Lingmell
2 Scafell Pike
3 Broad Crag
4 Ill Crag
5 Blunt Top
6 Scafell
7 Slight Side
8 Great End
9 Sprinkling Crags
10 Allen Crags
11 Glaramara
12 Looking Stead
13 Lincombe Tarns
14 Dovenest Top
15 Esk Pike
16 Bowfell
17 Bowfell North
18 Rossett Pike
19 High Raise
20 Thunacar Knott
21 Harrison Stickle
22 Pike o' Stickle
23 Loft Crag
24 Ullscarf
25 Crinkle Crags
26 Flesk
27 Shelter Crags
28 Cold Pike
29 Pike o' Blisco

SCAFELL GROUP

SCAFELL GROUP

Name	Height feet	metres	Maps 1" 2½" T	Grid Ref.	County
Lingmell	2649	807	82 NY20 T	209081	Cumberland
Scafell Pike[1]	3210[2]	978	82 NY20 T	215072	Cumberland
Broad Crag	3054[6]	931	82 NY20 T	219075	Cumberland
Ill Crag	3025+[3]	922+	82 NY20 T	223074	Cumberland
Blunt Top[4]	2950+	899+	82 NY20 T	224078	Cumberland
Scafell	3162	964	82 NY20 T	206064	Cumberland
Slight Side	2499	762	82 NY20 T	209050	Cumberland
Great End	2984[5]	910	82 NY20 T	226083	Cumberland
Sprinkling Crags[7]	2025+	617+	82 NY20 T	c.227095	Cumberland
Allen Crags	2572	784	82 NY20 T	236085	Cumberland
Glaramara	2560	780	82 NY21 T	247105	Cumberland
Looking Stead[8]	2550+	777+	82 NY21 T	245101	Cumberland
Lincombe Tarns[9]	2360[6]	719	82 NY20 T	242097	Cumberland
Dovenest Top[10]	2025+	617+	82 NY21 T	256113	Cumberland
Esk Pike	2903	885	82 NY20 T	236075	Cumberland
Bowfell	2960	902	82 NY20 T	244064	Cumberland and Westmorland
Bowfell North	2825	861	82 NY20 T	244070	Cumberland and Westmorland
Rossett Pike	2135[6]	651	82 NY20 T	249075	Cumberland and Westmorland
High Raise (summit = High White Stones)[6]	2500	762	82 NY20 T	280095	Cumberland[11]
Thunacar Knott	2362[6]	720	82 NY20 T	279080	Cumberland and Westmorland
Harrison Stickle	2403	732	82 NY20 T	281073	Westmorland
Pike o' Stickle[12]	2323	708	82 NY20 T	274073	Westmorland

Position	Best Ascended From	No. in order of Altitude		Date Ascended
		Sep. Mtn.	Top	
2 mi. ENE of Wast Water	Wasdale Head, $1\frac{1}{4}$ mi. to W	55	81	
2 mi. E of Wast Water	Wasdale Head, 2 mi. to NW; Seathwaite, $3\frac{1}{4}$ mi. to NNE	8	8	
$2\frac{1}{2}$ mi. E of Wast Water	Wasdale Head, 2 mi. to WNW	-	15	
$2\frac{1}{2}$ mi. E of Wast Water	Wasdale Head, $2\frac{1}{4}$ mi. to WNW	-	20	
$2\frac{3}{4}$ mi. E of Wast Water	Wasdale Head, $2\frac{1}{2}$ mi. to W	-	26	
$1\frac{3}{4}$ mi. ESE of Wast Water	Wasdale Head (head of Lake), $1\frac{3}{4}$ mi. to WNW	10	10	
$2\frac{1}{4}$ mi. SE of Wast Water	Head of Wast Water, $2\frac{1}{4}$ mi. to NW	-	130	
3 mi. ENE of Wast Water	Wasdale Head, $2\frac{1}{4}$ mi. to W; Seathwaite, $2\frac{1}{2}$ mi. to N	19	22	
$3\frac{1}{4}$ mi. NE of Wast Water	Seathwaite, $1\frac{3}{4}$ mi. to NW	-	374	
$3\frac{1}{2}$ mi. ENE of Wast Water	Seathwaite, $2\frac{1}{4}$ mi. to N	69	105	
2 mi. S of Seatoller	Seathwaite, $1\frac{1}{4}$ mi. to NW	72	109	
$2\frac{1}{4}$ mi. S of Seatoller	Seathwaite, $1\frac{1}{4}$ mi. to NNW	-	112	
$2\frac{1}{2}$ mi. S of Seatoller	Seathwaite, $1\frac{1}{2}$ mi. to NNW	-	172	
$1\frac{1}{2}$ mi. SE of Seatoller	Seathwaite, $1\frac{1}{4}$ mi. to WNW	-	373	
4 mi. S of Seatoller	Old Hotel, Langdale, $3\frac{1}{4}$ mi. to ESE	29	35	
$4\frac{3}{4}$ mi. W of Chapel Stile	Old Hotel, Langdale, $2\frac{1}{2}$ mi. to E	21	25	
$4\frac{3}{4}$ mi. W of Chapel Stile	Old Hotel, Langdale, $2\frac{1}{2}$ mi. to E	-	47	
$4\frac{1}{2}$ mi. WNW of Chapel Stile	Old Hotel, Langdale, $2\frac{1}{2}$ mi. to ESE	-	305	
$3\frac{1}{2}$ mi. NW of Chapel Stile	New Hotel, Langdale, 2 mi. to SSE	85	128	
3 mi. NW of Chapel Stile	New Hotel, Langdale, $1\frac{1}{4}$ mi. to SE	-	171	
$2\frac{3}{4}$ mi. NW of Chapel Stile	New Hotel, Langdale, 1 mi. to SE	-	159	
3 mi. WNW of Chapel Stile	New Hotel, Langdale $1\frac{1}{2}$ mi. to SE	-	192	

Loft Crag[13]	c.2270[14] c.692	82 NY20 T	277071	Westmorland
Ullscarf	2370	722	82 NY21 T	291121	Cumberland
Crinkle Crags[15]	2816	858	88 NY20 T	248048	Cumberland[16]
Flesk[17]	2733	833	88 NY20 T	249045	Cumberland and Westmorland
Shelter Crags	2667[6]	813	82 NY20 T	249054	Cumberland and Westmorland
Cold Pike	2259[18]	689	88 NY20 T	264035	Cumberland and Westmorland
Pike o' Blisco[19]	2304	702	88 NY20 T	270042	Westmorland

Notes

[1] Scafell Pikes on O.S. maps. Cumberland County Top.

[2] Estimated height under centre of cairn, according to a letter from the O.S. of 1971 November 2. Further, the height at the edge of the cairn is determined as 3209, and at the base of the triangulation pillar, 3206, as given on the 1970 edition of the One-inch Tourist Map.

[3] From $2\frac{1}{2}$" Map contours.

[4] Author's temporary name.

[5] But contours are shown on the $2\frac{1}{2}$" Map up to 3075 feet!

[6] Six-inch Map.

[7] Six-inch Map. "Seathwaite Crags" (Elmslie, Simpson).

[8] Six-inch Map. The west sides of both this top and Glaramara summit are there referred to as "Looking Steads". Also "Glaramara W. Centre Top" in Simpson's list.

[9] Author's temporary name, from several tarns of this name shown nearby on the Six-inch Map. Also "Glaramara S. Top" (Simpson).

[10] Author's temporary name, from crag name nearby. "Rosthwaite Fell" of Elmslie's list, and "Cam Crag" of Simpson's.

[11] But Westmorland very close indeed.

[12] "Pike _of_ Stickle" on O.S. maps.

[13] Simpson's alternative name "Thorn Crag" refers to a crag nearly half a mile to the E.

[14] Wainwright (3 Loft Crag 1).

56

$2\frac{3}{4}$ mi. WNW of Chapel Stile	Old Hotel, Langdale, $\frac{3}{4}$ mi. to SE	-	215
$4\frac{1}{2}$ mi. NNW of Chapel Stile	Stonethwaite, 2 mi. to NW	112	169
$4\frac{1}{2}$ mi. W of Chapel Stile	Old Hotel, Langdale, $2\frac{1}{4}$ mi. to ENE	35	48
$4\frac{1}{4}$ mi. W of Chapel Stile	Old Hotel, Langdale, $2\frac{1}{4}$ mi. to ENE	-	64
$4\frac{1}{2}$ mi. W of Chapel Stile	Old Hotel, Langdale, $2\frac{1}{4}$ mi. to ENE	-	78
$3\frac{3}{4}$ mi. WSW of Chapel Stile	Wrynose Pass, $\frac{3}{4}$ mi. to SE	-	222
3 mi. WSW of Chapel Stile	Old Hotel, Langdale, $1\frac{1}{4}$ mi. to NE	133	199

[15] "Crinkle Crags Long Top" (Simpson).

[16] Westmorland very close indeed.

[17] Six-inch Map. "Crinkle Crags S Top" in Simpson's list.

[18] Could be as high as 2280 feet according to Wainwright (4 Cold Pike 2).

[19] "Pike of Blisco" on O.S. maps.

[20] Cumberland very close indeed.

Scafell Range seen up Eskdale

CONISTON GROUP

Name	Height		Maps	Grid	County
	feet	metres	1" 2½" T	Ref.	
Harter Fell	2143[1]	653	88 SD29 T	218997	Cumberland
Grey Friar	2536	773	88 NY20 T	259003	Lancashire
Swirl How	2630	802	88 NY20 T	272005	Lancashire
Great Carrs	2575[2]	785	88 NY20 T	270008	Lancashire
Wetherlam (summit = Little Walls[6])	2502	763	88 NY20 T	288011	Lancashire
Black Sails[3]	2443	745	88 NY20 T	283007	Lancashire
The Old Man of Coniston[4]	2631	802	88 SD29 T	272978	Lancashire
Brim Fell	2611	796	88 SD29 T	270985	Lancashire
Dow Crag[5]	2555	779	88 SD29 T	262978	Lancashire
Walna Scar	2035[6]	620	88 SD29 T	258963	Lancashire
White Maiden[6]	2000+	610+	88 SD29 T	253957	Lancashire

<u>Notes</u>

[1] According to a letter from the O.S. of 1971 November 2, this is the height of the summit. The altitude 2129 given on the 1970 edition of the O.S. One-inch Tourist Map is that at the base of the triangulation pillar.

[2] Wainwright (4 Great Carrs 1).

[3] "Wetherlam W. Top" (Simpson).

[4] Also known as "Coniston Old Man" or just "The Old Man". Lancashire County Top.

[5] Sometimes spelt "Doe Crag", but this appears to be incorrect.

[6] Six-inch Map.

Position	Best Ascended From	No. in order of Altitude		Date Asc- ended
		Sep. Mtn.	Top	
$5\frac{1}{4}$ mi. WNW of Coniston	Hard Knott Pass, $1\frac{1}{4}$ mi. to NE; Troutal, $1\frac{1}{4}$ mi. to SE	193	301	
3 mi. NW of Coniston	Cockley Beck, 1 mi. to NW	77	115	
$2\frac{1}{2}$ mi. NW of Coniston	Wrynose Pass, $1\frac{1}{4}$ mi. to N	62	89	
$2\frac{3}{4}$ mi. NW of Coniston	Wrynose Pass, 1 mi. to NNE	-	104	
$2\frac{1}{4}$ mi. NNW of Coniston	Fell Foot, $1\frac{1}{2}$ mi. to NNE	84	126	
$2\frac{1}{4}$ mi. NNW of Coniston	Fell Foot, $1\frac{3}{4}$ mi. to NNE	-	145	
$1\frac{3}{4}$ mi. W of Coniston	Coniston, $1\frac{3}{4}$ mi. to E	60	87	
2 mi. W of Coniston	Coniston, 2 mi. to E	-	94	
$2\frac{1}{2}$ mi. W of Coniston	Troutal, $1\frac{3}{4}$ mi. to WNW; Torver, $2\frac{1}{2}$ mi. to SE	74	111	
3 mi. WSW of Coniston	Seathwaite, $1\frac{1}{2}$ mi. to W	-	365	
$3\frac{1}{4}$ mi. WSW of Coniston	Seathwaite, $1\frac{1}{2}$ mi. to W	-	407	

Langdale Pikes from Elterwater Village

For many centuries now the Cheviot Hills have formed the principal barrier between the nations of England and Scotland, and to this day the people living immediately to north and south of it have scarcely any social contact. The barrier ridge of the Cheviots rises steadily towards the east where it culminates in a large dome-shaped massif. There are eight "two-thousanders" in the Cheviots, all of them being in the area of this dome.

The nearest towns are Wooler and Kelso but almost more important to hill-walkers is the village of Kirk Yetholm, since it is the northern terminus of the Pennine Way, which traverses or visits four "twos" in the Cheviots: Windy Gyle, Hangingstone Hill, The Cheviot and Auchope Cairn.

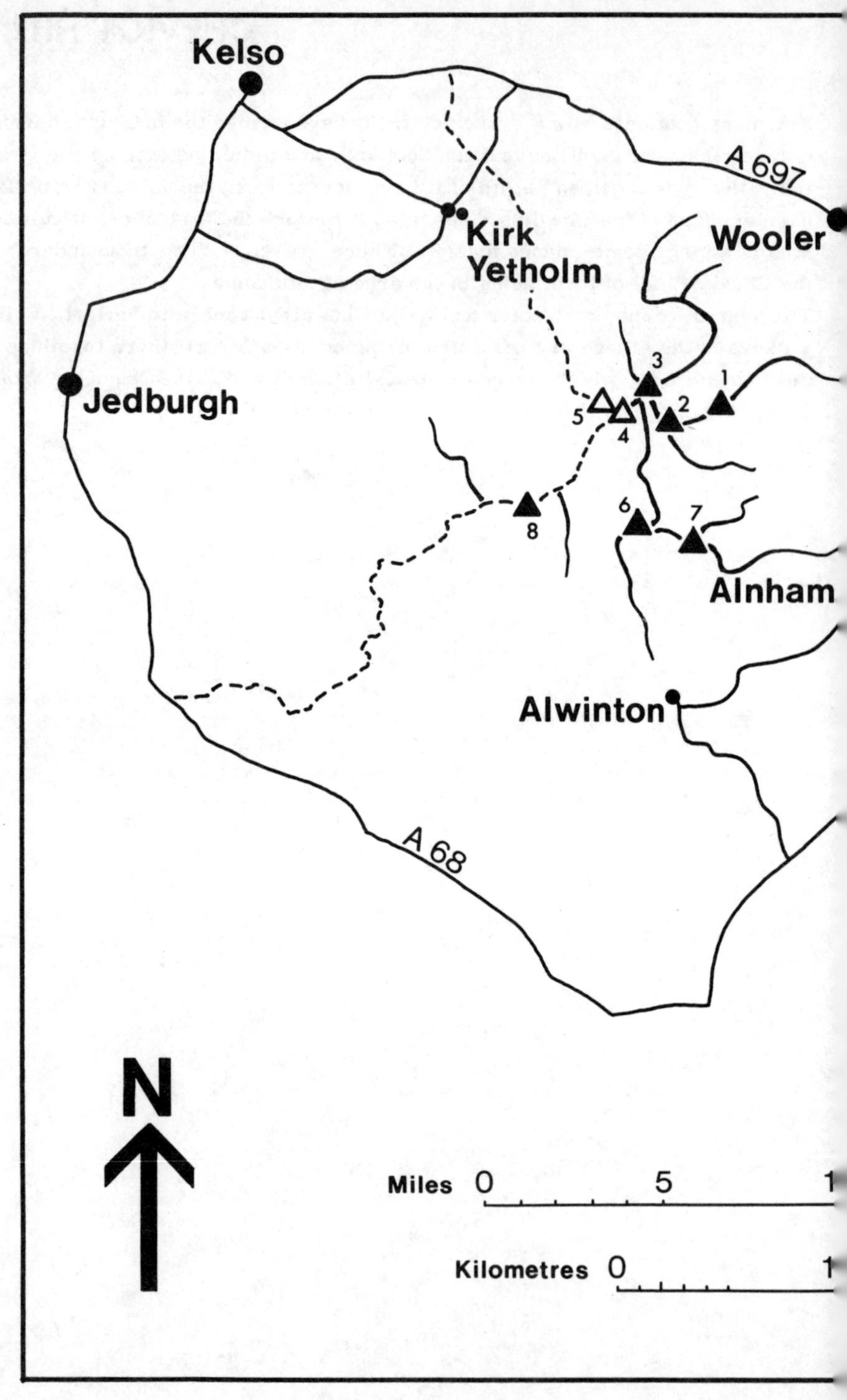

Kelso
Kirk Yetholm
Wooler
A 697
Jedburgh
3
1
2
5
4
6
7
8
Alnham
Alwinton
A 68
N
Miles 0 5 1
Kilometres 0 1

THE CHEVIOTS

1 Hedgehope Hill
2 Comb Fell
3 The Cheviot
4 Hangingstone Hill
5 Auchope Cairn
6 Bloodybush Edge
7 Cushat Law
8 Windy Gyle

▲ **Separate Mountain**　　　　△**Subsidiary Mountain**

Name	Height		Maps	Grid	County
	feet	metres	1" 2½" T	Ref.	
Hedgehope Hill	2343	714	71 NT91	943197	Northumberland
Comb Fell	2132	650	71 NT91	918186	Northumberland
The Cheviot[1]	2674	815	71 NT92	909205	Northumberland
Hangingstone Hill[2]	2433[6]	742	70 NT81	895193	Northumberland and Roxburghshire
Auchope Cairn[3]	2382	726	70 NT81	891198	Northumberland and Roxburghshire
Bloodybush Edge	2001	610	71 NT91	902143	Northumberland
Cushat Law	2020	616	71 NT91	928137	Northumberland
Windy Gyle[4] (summit = Russell's Cairn)	2032	619	70 NT81	855152	Northumberland and Roxburghshire

<u>Notes</u>

[1] Northumberland County Top.

[2] Author's temporary name, from a feature called Hanging Stone a few hundred yards to the SW of the summit (Six-inch Map). Also = "Point SE" of E. Moss's list.

[3] Decided from 1:2500 (2½") Map contours. Technically the actual summit is a few yards on the Roxburghshire side of the boundary.

[4] Also = "Windygate Hill" in Elmslie's list.

[6] Six-inch Map.

Position	Best Ascended From	No. in order of Altitude		Date Ascended
		Sep. Mtn.	Top	
6 mi. SW of Wooler	Longleeford, 1½ mi. to NNE	118	179	
7½ mi. SW of Wooler	Longleeford, 3 mi. to NE	195	307	
7 mi. SW of Wooler	Longleeford, 2½ mi. to ENE	53	77	
7 mi. SE of Kirk Yetholm	Cocklawfoot, 2¾ mi. to WSW	-	147	
6½ mi. SE of Kirk Yetholm	Cocklawfoot, 2½ mi. to WSW	-	163	
10 mi. SW of Wooler	Alwinton, 5 mi. to SSE	243	395	
10 mi. SSW of Wooler	Alwinton, 4½ mi. to S; Alnam, 4½ mi. to SE	232	377	
8¼ mi. SSE of Kirk Yetholm	Cocklawfoot, 2 mi. to N	228	367	

The Pennine Range, sometimes called the Pennine Chain or more usually, and simply, The Pennines, is a broad barrier of high ground thrusting down through northern England and confining the lower ground on each side to the dimensions of a narrow coastal plain. It is a complete region in itself, being 140 miles long, seldom less than twenty miles wide, and rising nearly everywhere to levels between 1500 and 2500 feet in altitude. However, it is by no means a monolithic massif, and the chain-like character of the range is well in evidence in the main part of the range as well as in its numerous subsidiary branches. Moreover, of the several passes and gaps and valleys which at intervals all but sever the main chain, two mark important changes of mountain structure and scenery. These are the Stainmore Forest pass, which separates the Northern Pennines from the Central groups, and the Aire Gap, which separates the Central region from the Southern Pennines. Altogether there are 79 two-thousanders in the Pennine Range.

NORTHERN PENNINES

The fells of the Northern Pennines comprise a more nearly single block of high ground than those of any other part of the range. Indeed, they present to the west one of the greatest sights in the Pennines - a formidable scarp which for thirty miles runs practically unbroken. Only in the east and north does the high ground descend gently to long lonely valleys whose rivers have cut back deeply into the massif. Thirty-seven of the peaks rise above 2,000 feet and the Pennine Way traverses four of them -Knock Fell, the Great and Little Dun Fells, and Cross Fell -and passes close to two others: Backstone Edge and Longman Hill. Cross Fell is the highest mountain in the Pennines and the highest in England outside the Lake District.
Two of the few roads in the region conveniently divide it into more manageable units. These are the Alston-Penrith road (A 686), to the north of which lie the three summits of the Black Fell group; and the Alston-Barnard Castle road (B 6277), which separates the fells of the Burnhope Seat group from those above which Cross Fell presides.
The nearest towns are Alston, Appleby and Middleton in Teesdale.

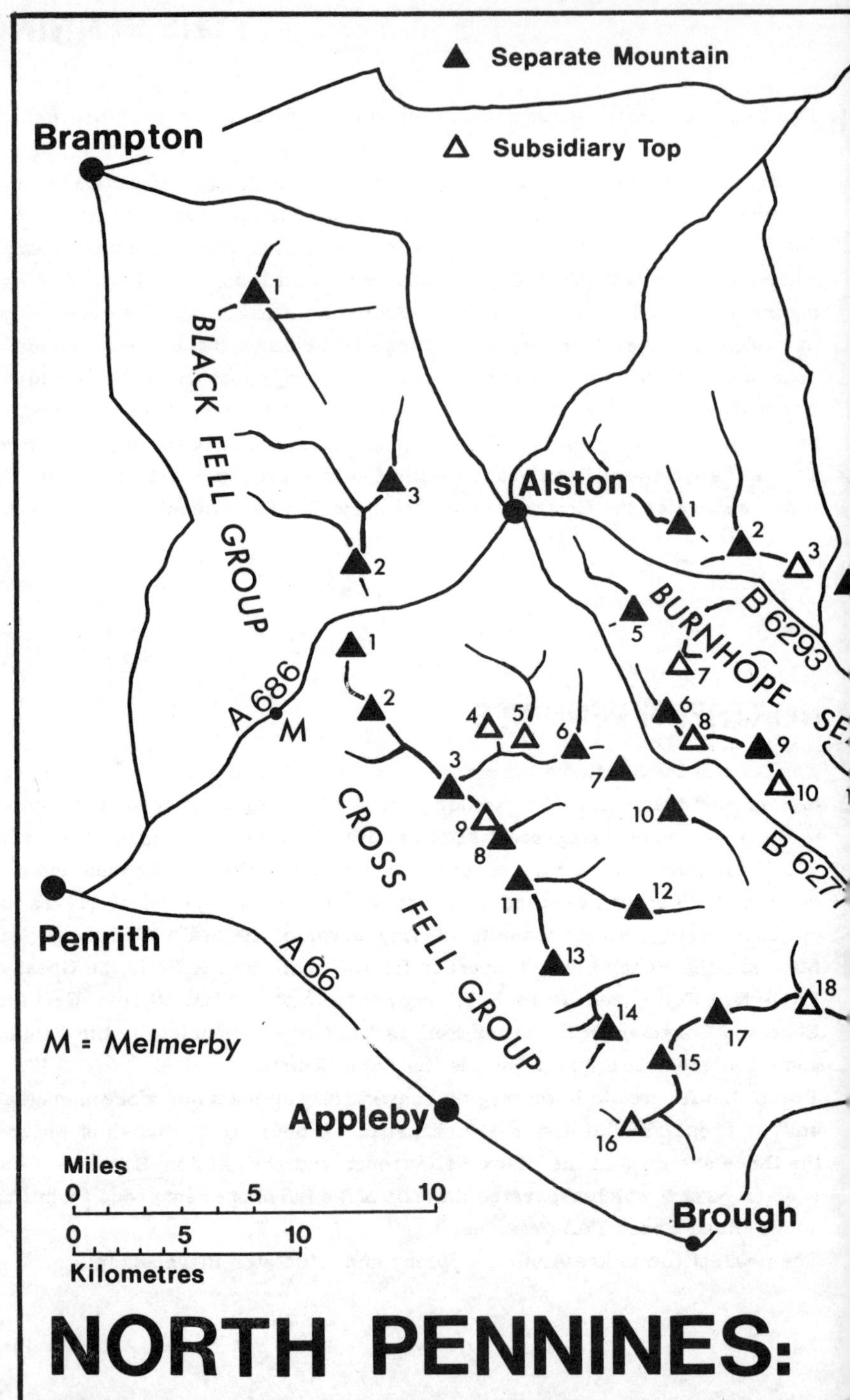

NORTH PENNINES:

BURNHOPE SEAT GROUP

1 The Dodd
2 Killhope Law
3 Stangend Rigg
4 Middlehope Moor
5 Flinty Fell
6 Burnhope Seat
7 Dead Stones
8 Redgleam
9 High Field
10 Three Pikes
11 Chapelfell Top
12 Fendrith Hill
13 James's Hill
14 Black Hill
15 Outberry Plain

CROSS FELL GROUP

1 Fiend's Fell
2 Melmerby Fell
3 Cross Fell
4 Bullman Hills
5 Long Man Hill
6 Round Hill
7 Bellbeaver Rigg
8 Great Dun Fell
9 Little Dun Fell
10 Viewing Hill
11 Knock Fell
12 Meldon Hill
13 Backstone Edge
14 Murton Fell
15 Little Fell
16 Long Fell
17 Mickle Fell
18 Long Crag
19 Rink Moss

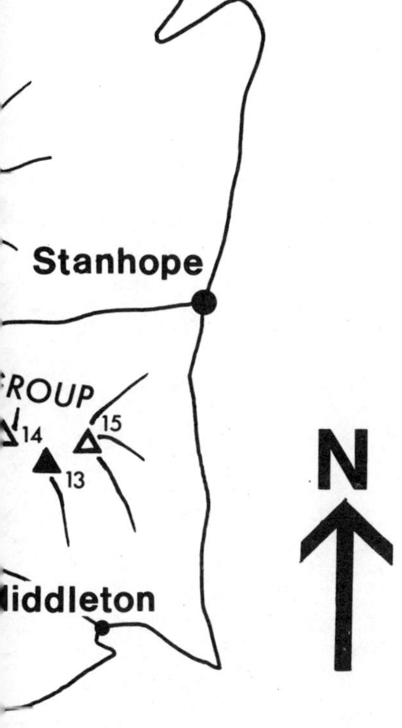

BLACK FELL GROUP
BURNHOPE SEAT GROUP
CROSS FELL GROUP

BLACK FELL GROUP

Name	Height feet metres		Maps 1" 2½" T	Grid Ref.	County
Cold Fell	2037	621	76 NY65	605556	Cumberland
Black Fell	2179	664	83 NY64	648444	Cumberland
Grey Nag[1] (<u>summit</u> = <u>Middle Currick</u>[6])	2153	656	83 NY64	664476	Northumberland

<u>Notes</u>

[1] Also: Thornton Carrs.

[6] Six-inch Map.

Position	Best Ascended From	No. in order of Altitude		Date Ascended
		Sep. Mtn.	Top	
$5\frac{3}{4}$ mi. SE of Brampton	Forest Head, $1\frac{3}{4}$ mi. to NW	225	359	
$4\frac{1}{2}$ mi. WSW of Alston	Hartside Cross, $1\frac{1}{2}$ mi. to S	178	274	
$3\frac{1}{4}$ mi. WNW of Alston	Castle Nook, 2 mi. to ENE	189	293	

BURNHOPE SEAT GROUP

Name	Height feet	metres	Maps 1" 2½" T	Grid Ref.	County
The Dodd	2013	614	84 NY74	791458	Northumberland[1]
Killhope Law	2207	673	84 NY84	819448	Durham and Northumberland
Stangend Rigg[2]	2075	632	84 NY84	841436	Durham[3]
Middlehope Moor[4]	2000+	610+	84 NY84	867429 & 862432	Durham and Northumberland
Flinty Fell	2013	614	84 NY74	771419	Cumberland
Burnhope Seat[5]	2452	747	84 NY73	785375	Cumberland[5]
Dead Stones	2326	709	84 NY73	793398	Cumberland and Durham
Redgleam[7]	2342	714	84 NY73	795362	Durham
High Field[6]	2322	708	84 NY83	823359	Durham
Three Pikes	2133	650	84 NY83	834343	Durham
Chapelfell Top	2297[6]	700	84 NY83	875346	Durham
Fendrith Hill	2284	696	84 NY83	876333	Durham
James's Hill[8]	2216	675	84 NY93	923325	Durham
Black Hill	2115	645	84 NY93	906334	Durham
Outberry Plain[9]	2150+	655+	84 NY93	c.938330	Durham

Notes

[1] Cumberland is very close indeed.

[2] Six-inch Map. "Stangend Currick" (E. Moss).

[3] Northumberland is very close indeed.

[4] Twin summits. Called "Allenheads" by Docharty.

[5] Durham is very close ineeed;   230 yards to the E, on the boundary, is Durham's County Top, (unnamed).

Position	Best Ascended From	No. in order of Altitude		Date Ascended
		Sep. Mtn.	Top	
$4\frac{3}{4}$ mi. E of Alston	Nenthead, $1\frac{1}{4}$ mi. to S	336	382	
$6\frac{1}{2}$ mi. E of Alston	Unclassified road, $\frac{3}{4}$ mi. to N	164	253	
10 mi. WNW of Stanhope	Point 1829 on B6295 road, $\frac{3}{4}$ mi. to E	-	335	
8 mi. WNW of Stanhope	Point 1829 on B6295 road, 1 mi. to W	246	400	
$4\frac{1}{2}$ mi. SE of Alston	Dowgang Hush, $\frac{1}{2}$ mi. to N	235	381	
$7\frac{1}{4}$ mi. SE of Alston	Darngill Bridge, $\frac{3}{4}$ mi. to WSW	95	142	
$6\frac{1}{2}$ mi. SE of Alston	Killhope Cross, 2 mi. to N	-	190	
8 mi. SE of Alston	B6277 road, $\frac{3}{4}$ mi. to S	-	180	
$9\frac{1}{2}$ mi. SE of Alston	Rough Rigg, 1 mi. to S	128	193	
10 mi. WSW of Stanhope	Rough Rigg, 1 mi. to W	-	306	
8 mi. WSW of Stanhope	Point 2056 on unclassified road, $\frac{3}{4}$ mi. to W	136	204	
8 mi. WSW of Stanhope	Swinhope Head, $1\frac{1}{4}$ mi. to E	-	211	
6 mi. SW of Stanhope	Swinhope Head, $1\frac{1}{2}$ mi. to WNW	158	246	
$6\frac{1}{2}$ mi. SW of Stanhope	Swinhope Head, $\frac{1}{2}$ mi. to W	-	314	
5 mi. SW of Stanhope	Unclassified road, $2\frac{1}{2}$ mi. to S	-	295	

[6] Six-inch Map

[7] "Ashgill Head" (Elmslie); "Harwood Common" (E. Moss).

[8] Six-inch Map. Also: Newbiggin Common, Westernhope Moor (Elmslie), Hudeshope Fell (Docharty), and "Outberry Plain West Top" (E. Moss).

[9] "Outberry Plain East Top" (E. Moss).

CROSS FELL GROUP

Name	Height feet	metres	Maps 1" 2½" T	Grid Ref.	County
Fiend's Fell [1]	2079	634	83 NY64	643406	Cumberland
Melmerby Fell (<u>summit</u>= <u>Dun Edge</u>)	2331	710	83 NY63	652380	Cumberland
Cross Fell [2]	2930	893	83 NY63	687343	Cumberland
Bullman Hills [3]	2002	610	83 NY73	705373	Cumberland
Long Man Hill	2160	658	83 NY73	723372	Cumberland
Round Hill [4]	2249	685	84 NY73	744361	Cumberland
Bellbeaver Rigg	2035	620	84 NY73	762351	Cumberland
Great Dun Fell [5]	2780	847	83 NY73	710321	Westmorland
Little Dun Fell [5]	2761	842	83 NY73	704330	Westmorland
Viewing Hill [7]	2111[6]	643	84 NY73	786334	Durham
Knock Fell [8]	2604	794	83 NY73	721302	Westmorland
Meldon Hill [9]	2518	767	84 NY72	771290	Westmorland
Backstone Edge	2292	699	83 NY72	725276	Westmorland
Murton Fell [10]	2207	673	84 NY72	758240	Westmorland
Little Fell [11]	2446	746	84 NY72	781224 & 784217	Westmorland
Long Fell	2035[6]	620	84 NY71	768198	Westmorland
Mickle Fell [12]	2591	790	84 NY82	805245	Yorkshire (North Riding)
Long Crag	2250+	686+	84 NY82	842252	Yorkshire (North Riding)
Bink Moss	2028	618	84 NY82	876242	Yorkshire (North Riding)

Position	Best Ascended From	No. in order of Altitude		Date Asc-ended
		Sep. Mtn.	Top	
$1\frac{3}{4}$ mi. NE of Melmerby	Hartside Cross, $\frac{3}{4}$ mi. to NNE	208	332	
$2\frac{1}{4}$ mi. ENE of Melmerby	Hartside Cross, $2\frac{1}{4}$ mi. to N	123	186	
5 mi. ESE of Melmerby	Kirkland, $2\frac{3}{4}$ mi. to WSW	24	29	
$5\frac{3}{4}$ mi. S of Alston	Leadgate, 4 mi. to N	-	393	
$5\frac{1}{2}$ mi. S of Alston	Garrigill, 3 mi. to NNE	-	286	
6 mi. SSE of Alston	Hill House, $1\frac{1}{2}$ mi. to NNE	150	231	
7 mi. SSE of Alston	Hill House, $2\frac{1}{4}$ mi. to NNW	227	361	
$6\frac{3}{4}$ mi. SE of Melmerby	Milburn, 4 mi. to SW	41	54	
$6\frac{1}{4}$ mi. ESE of Melmerby	Milburn, $3\frac{3}{4}$ mi. to SW	-	57	
$11\frac{1}{2}$ mi. N of Brough	Point 1947 on B. 6277 road, $1\frac{1}{4}$ mi. to N	199	315	
$6\frac{1}{2}$ mi. NNE of Appleby	Knock, $3\frac{1}{4}$ mi. to SW	66	96	
9 mi. N of Brough	Hilton, $5\frac{1}{2}$ mi. to SSW	81	121	
5 mi. NNE of Appleby	Dufton, $2\frac{1}{2}$ mi. to SW	137	205	
6 mi. NNW of Brough	Hilton, $2\frac{1}{2}$ mi. to SW	166	255	
5 mi. NNW of Brough	Hilton, 3 mi. to WSW	97	144	
$3\frac{1}{2}$ mi. NNW of Brough	Hilton, $2\frac{1}{4}$ mi. to W	-	363	
6 mi. N of Brough	B. 6276 road, $3\frac{1}{4}$ mi. to SSE	68	101	
$7\frac{1}{4}$ mi. NE of Brough	Langdon Beck, $3\frac{3}{4}$ mi. to NNE	-	227	
$7\frac{3}{4}$ mi. NE of Brough	Hargill Bridge, $1\frac{3}{4}$ mi. to S	229	370	

<u>Notes</u>

[1] Also: Gamblesby Allotments.

[2] The source of the River Tees is on this fell to the E.

[3] Twin summits, the lower one being 2000+ in altitude, at 704370.

[4] The source of the River South Tyne is on this fell to the SE.

[5] "Milburn Forest" (Elmslie).

[6] Six-inch Map.

[7] Also: Herdship Fell.

[8] Also: Green Fell and The Heights.

[9] Also: Dufton Fell (Docharty, Elmslie and E. Moss).

[10] Another summit at 2206 is about a mile to the NNW, at 750255.

[11] Twin summits about $\frac{1}{2}$ mile apart. Also known as Hilton Fell (Elmslie).

[12] Yorkshire (North Riding) County Top.

DANGER - Little Fell, Long Fell and Mickle Fell. An artillery range occupies a substantial area of countryside in these regions.   Enquire locally about access and the times of firing.

CENTRAL PENNINES

Between the Stainmore Forest and the Aire Gap, the Central Pennines form
a complicated system of isolated peaks and ridges separated by a maze of deep
trough-shaped valleys. The peaks here have an individuality and shapeliness
greater than usual among the Pennine hills, and they are consequently held in
high regard by mountaineers. Indeed, one of them, Ingleborough, has been
described as the most interesting mountain in England; and, together with
Whernside and Penyghent, it carries the course of the famous Three Peaks
Walk. There are thirty-nine tops in the region, three of which are traversed
by the Pennine Way - Fountains Fell, Penyghent and Great Shunner Fell -
which also passes close to three others: Darnbrook Fell, Plover Hill and
Dodd Fell Hill.

Wensleydale is the major river valley in this region, and together with the
much shorter Garsdale in the west it offers a convenient boundary between the
Great Shunner group of fells to the north, and the Ingleborough group to its
south.

The principal towns are Settle, Ingleton, Sedbergh and Kirkby Stephen. Well-
known and much-loved villages include Malham, Grassington, Horton, Hawes,
Kettlewell and Litton. A very famous isolated public house, the Tan Hill, is
in the extreme north of the region.

Ingleborough from the North

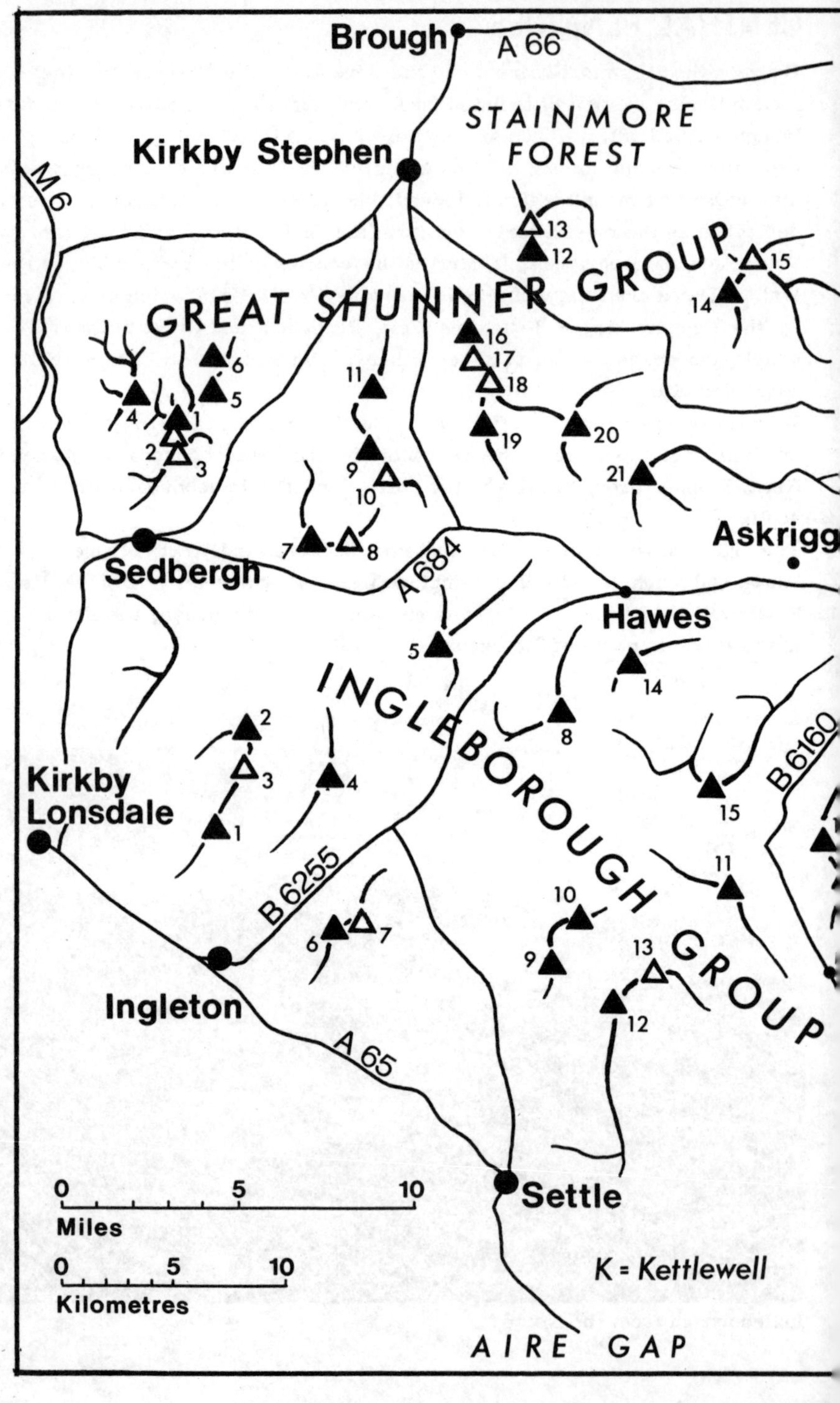

Brough
A 66
Kirkby Stephen
STAINMORE FOREST
M 6
13
12
15
14
GREAT SHUNNER GROUP
6
5
4
1
2
3
11
16
17
18
19
20
9
10
7
8
21
Askrigg
Sedbergh
A 684
Hawes
5
14
INGLEBOROUGH GROUP
2
3
4
1
8
Kirkby Lonsdale
B 6255
B 6160
15
11
10
6
7
9
13
12
Ingleton
A 65
0   5   10
Miles
0   5   10
Kilometres
Settle
K = Kettlewell
AIRE GAP

CENTRAL PENNINES:

GREAT SHUNNER GROUP
INGLEBOROUGH GROUP

GREAT SHUNNER GROUP

1 The Calf
2 Bram Rigg Top
3 Calders
4 Fell Head
5 Yarlside
6 Randygill Top
7 Knoutberry Haw
8 Tarn Rigg Hill
9 Swarth Fell

10 Swarth Fell Pike
11 Wild Boar Fell
12 White Mossy Hill
13 Nine Standards Rigg
14 Rogan's Seat
15 Water Crag
16 High Seat
17 Archy Styrigg
18 Hugh Seat
19 Sails
20 Great Shunner Fell
21 Lovely Seat

INGLEBOROUGH GROUP

1 Gragareth
2 Great Coum
3 Green Hill
4 Whernside
5 Great Knoutberry Hill
6 Ingleborough Hill
7 Simon Fell
8 Dodd Fell Hill
9 Penyghent Hill
10 Plover Hill
11 Birks Fell
12 Fountains Fell
13 Darnbrook Fell
14 Drumaldrace
15 Yockenthwaite Moor
16 Buckden Pike
17 Tor Mere Top
18 Great Whernside

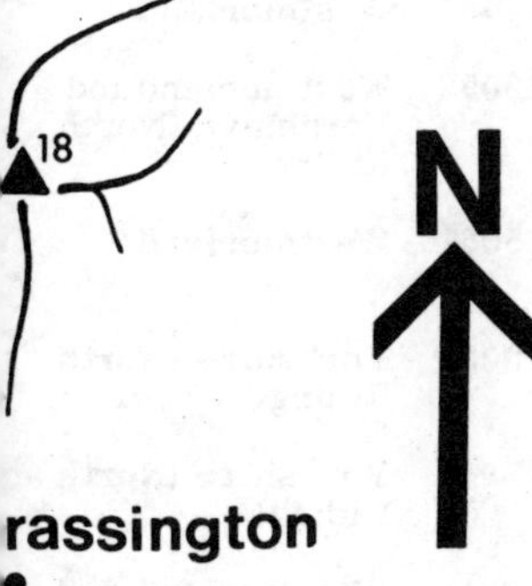

▲ **Separate Mountain**

△ **Subsidiary Mountain**

GREAT SHUNNER GROUP

Name	Height feet	metres	Maps 1" 2½" T	Grid Ref.	County
The Calf	2219	676	89 SD69	667970	Westmorland and Yorkshire (West Riding)
Bram Rigg Top	2200+	671+	89 SD69	668965	Yorkshire (West Riding)
Calders	2200+	671+	89 SD69	670960	Yorkshire (West Riding)
Fell Head	2050+	625+	89 SD69	c.650984	Yorkshire (West Riding)
Yarlside	2097	639	89 SD69	685985	Westmorland
Randygill Top	2047	624	89 NY60	686000	Westmorland
Knoutberry Haw [1]	2216	675	90 SD79	731919	Yorkshire (West Riding)
Tarn Rigg Hill	2200+	671+	90 SD79	742916	Yorkshire (West Riding)
Swarth Fell	2235	681	90 SD79	755966	Westmorland [2]
Swarth Fell Pike [3]	2125 [6]	648	90 SD79	760958	Westmorland and Yorkshire (West Riding) [4]
Wild Boar Fell	2324	708	90 SD79	757987	Westmorland
White Mossy Hill [5]	2175+	663+	84 NY80	828052	Westmorland and Yorkshire (North Riding)
Nine Standards Rigg	2171	662	84 NY80	825061	Westmorland [7]
Rogan's Seat	2203	671	90 NY90	919030	Yorkshire (North Riding)
Water Crag	2188	667	90 NY90	928046	Yorkshire (North Riding)
High Seat	2328	710	90 NY80	802012	Westmorland and Yorkshire (North Riding)
Archy Styrigg (<u>summit = Gregory Chapel</u>) [8]	2250+	686+	90 NY80	802003	Westmorland and Yorkshire (North Riding

Position	Best Ascended From	No. in order of Altitude		Date Asc-ended
		Sep. Mtn.	Top	
3 mi. N of Sedbergh	"Hotel" on A. 683 road, 2 mi. to E	157	245	
2¾ mi. N of Sedbergh	"Hotel" on A. 683 road, 2 mi. to E.	-	260	
2½ mi. NNE of Sedbergh	"Hotel" on A. 683 road, 1¾ mi. to E	-	261	
4 mi. N of Sedbergh	Fairmile Gate, 1¼ mi. to W	219	347	
4 mi. NNE of Sedbergh	"Hotel" on A. 683 road, 1¼ mi. to SE	204	324	
5 mi. NNE of Sedbergh	"Hotel" on A. 683 road, 2 mi. to SSE	221	353	
9 mi. W of Hawes	Birkrigg, 1 mi. to SSW	159	247	
8 mi. W of Hawes	Thursgill, 1¼ mi. to SSE	-	264	
8¼ mi. NW of Hawes	Aisgill Moor Cottages, 1¼ mi. to E.	152	235	
7¾ mi. NW of Hawes	Aisgill Moor Cottages, 1 mi. to ENE	-	311	
4 mi. SE of Ravenstonedale	Hazelgill, 1½ mi. to NE	127	191	
4 mi. SE of Kirkby Stephen	Lamps Moss on B6270 road, 1¼ mi. to SW	181	277	
3½ mi. ESE of Kirkby Stephen	Lamps Moss on B. 6270 road, 1½ mi. to SW	-	280	
9½ mi. ESE of Kirkby Stephen	Keld, 2 mi. to SW	169	258	
9½ mi. ESE of Kirkby Stephen	Tan Hill Inn, 2¼ mi. to NW	-	270	
4½ mi. SE of Kirkby Stephen	Outhgill, 1¼ mi. to W	126	189	
5 mi. SE of Kirkby Stephen	Outhgill, 1½ mi. to NW	-	225	

Hugh Seat[9]	2257	688	89 SD89	809991	Westmorland and Yorkshire (North Riding
Sails[10]	2186	666	90 SD89	808965	Yorkshire (North Riding)
Great Shunner Fell	2340	713	90 SD89	848972	Yorkshire (North Riding
Lovely Seat	2213	675	90 SD89	879950	Yorkshire (North Riding)

Notes

[1] Also: Baugh Fell; and "East Baugh Fell" (E. Moss).

[2] Yorkshire (North Riding) and Yorkshire (West Riding) both very close indeed.

[3] Decided from 1:25000 Map contours; "Point SE" (E. Moss).

[4] Yorkshire (North Riding) very close indeed.

[5] Decided from 1:25000 ($2\frac{1}{2}$") Map contours.

[6] Six-inch Map.

[7] Yorkshire (North Riding) not far away.

[8] Both names from the Six-inch Map. "Point S" (E. Moss).

[9] Black Fell Moss (Elmslie).

[10] Ure Head (Elmslie and E. Moss) and Lunds Fell (E. Moss). The source of Wensleydale's river, the R. Ure, is on this fell.

6 mi. SE of Kirkby Stephen	Elmgill, $1\frac{1}{2}$ mi. to W	-	223
$5\frac{3}{4}$ mi. NW of Hawes	West End, $1\frac{1}{4}$ mi. to SW	175	271
$4\frac{3}{4}$ mi. NNW of Hawes	Thwaite, $2\frac{3}{4}$ mi. to ENE	119	181
$3\frac{1}{4}$ mi. N of Hawes	Point 1726 on unclassified road, $\frac{3}{4}$ mi. to NW	161	249

INGLEBOROUGH GROUP

Name	Height feet	metres	Maps 1"	2½" T	Grid Ref.	County
Gragareth [1]	2058	627	89	SD67	687793	Lancashire and Yorkshire (West Riding)
Great Coum	2250	686	90	SD78	700835	Yorkshire (West Riding) [2]
Green Hill [3]	2054	626	90	SD78	701814	Lancashire and Yorkshire (West Riding)
Whernside [4]	2419	737	90	SD78	738814	Yorkshire (West Riding)
Great Knoutberry Hill [5]	2203	671	90	SD78	788871	Yorkshire (North Riding) and Yorkshire (West Riding)
Ingleborough Hill	2373	723	90	SD77	741745	Yorkshire (West Riding)
Simon Fell	2100+	640+	90	SD77	c.753750	Yorkshire (West Riding)
Dodd Fell Hill	2189	667	90	SD88	840845	Yorkshire (North Riding) [7]
Penyghent Hill	2273	693	90	SD87	838733	Yorkshire (West Riding)
Plover Hill	2231	680	90	SD87	848752	Yorkshire (West Riding)
Birks Fell	2001	610	90	SD97	918763	Yorkshire (West Riding)
Fountains Fell	2191	668	90	SD87	864715	Yorkshire (West Riding)
Darnbrook Fell	2048	624	90	SD87	884727	Yorkshire (West Riding)
Drumaldrace [8]	2015	614	90	SD88	872867	Yorkshire (North Riding)
Yockenthwaite Moor [9]	2109	643	90	SD98	908810	Yorkshire (North Riding) and Yorkshire (West Riding)
Buckden Pike [10]	2302	702	90	SD97	960787	Yorkshire (North Riding) and Yorkshire (West Riding)
Tor Mere Top [11]	2050+	625+	90	SD97	969765	Yorkshire (North Riding) and Yorkshire (West Riding)

Position	Best Ascended From	No. in order of Altitude		Date Ascended
		Sep. Mtn.	Top	
8½ mi. SSE of Sedbergh	Unclassified road, 1¼ mi. to E	216	342	
6 mi. SE of Sedbergh	Unclassified road, ½ mi. to E	149	229	
7 mi. SSE of Sedbergh	Unclassified road, ½ mi. to E	-	346	
9½ mi. SW of Hawes	Unclassified road, 1 mi. to W	100	152	
5¼ mi. WSW of Hawes	Stone House, 1¼ mi. to SW	168	257	
3¼ mi. NE of Ingleton	Storrs Cave, 2½ mi. to SW	110	167	
4½ mi. NE of Ingleton	Selside, 2 mi. to ENE	-	322	
3¾ mi. SW of Hawes	Point 1857 on unclassified road, 1¼ mi. to E	174	269	
6 mi. NNE of Settle	Unclassified road, 1¼ mi. to SSE	141	214	
7½ mi. NNE of Settle	Unclassified road, 1 mi. to SE	154	237	
10 mi. NE of Settle	Buckden, 1½ mi. to ENE	242	394	
5½ mi. NE of Settle	Blishmire Close, 1 mi. to NW	173	268	
7 mi. NE of Settle	Blishmire Close, 2 mi. to W	-	351	
1¾ mi. S of Hawes	Point 1775 on unclassified road, 1 mi. to SW	234	380	
5¾ mi. SSE of Hawes	Yockenthwaite, 1¼ mi. to S	200	317	
9¼ mi. NNW of Grassington	Point 1376 on B6160 road, 1½ mi. to NW	134	200	
8 mi. NNW of Grassington	Starbotton, 1½ mi. to SW	-	349	

Great Whernside   2310   704   90 SE07   002739   Yorkshire (West
                                                                 Riding) [12]

Notes

[1] "Greygarth Hill" on Bartholomew's Half-Inch Map, and in Elmslie's list.

[2] Westmorland extremely close.

[3] Foul Moss (Elmslie).

[4] Yorkshire (West Riding) County Top.

[5] Also: Widdale Fell.

[7] Yorkshire (West Riding) not far away.

[8] Also: Wether Fell, and "Drumddrace" (E. Moss).

[9] Middle Tongue (E. Moss).

[10] Also: Buckden Gavel, (summit = Ramsden Pike); both names from old Six-inch Maps.

[11] Also: Starbotton Out Moor. Decided from 1:2500 Map contours.

[12] Yorkshire (North Riding) not far away.

SOUTHERN PENNINES

South of the Aire Gap the main range of the Pennines throws off a final spur of moorland westwards into Lancashire before diminishing to a narrow isthmus of high ground forming the watershed between the densely populated regions of South Lancashire and Yorkshire.   Farther south the range broadens out once again, and for the last time, as it rises to the high moorlands of the Peak District before finally descending, through a region of limestone uplands, to its last foothills somewhere in the neighbourhood of Ashbourne.   There are only three tops in this region, all of them being in the northern part of the Peak District.   The southernmost and highest of them is Kinder Scout, a large plateau cut off from its surroundings by steep scarps: surely the strangest mountain in the British Isles.   The Pennine Way, after leaving its southern terminus at Edale, traverses Kinder Scout and one of the other summits, Bleaklow Head, and passes close to the third, Higher Shelf Stones, in the first few miles of its 270-mile course.

The towns and villages nearest to this part of the Peak District include Edale, Hayfield, Glossop and Langsett.

PEAK DISTRICT

Name	Height feet metres		Maps 1" 2½" T[1]		Grid Ref.	County
Bleaklow[2] (<u>summits = Bleaklow Head and Bleaklow Stones</u>)	2060	628	102 SK09	T SK19	092959 115963	Derbyshire
Higher Shelf Stones	2039	621	102 SK09	T	089947	Derbyshire
Kinder Scout[3]	2088	636	102 SK08 111	T	086875	Derbyshire

<u>Notes</u>

[1] Peak District One-inch Tourist Map.

[2] The two summits are about 1½ miles apart and equal in altitude.

[3] Derbyshire County Top.

Position	Best Ascended From	No. in order of Altitude	Date Asc-ended
		Sep. Mtn.	Top
$3\frac{3}{4}$ and $5\frac{1}{4}$ mi. respectively ENE of Glossop	Snake Road A. 57, 2 mi. to S., and $2\frac{3}{4}$ mi. to SW	214	340
$3\frac{1}{4}$ mi. E of Glossop	Snake Road, A. 57, $1\frac{1}{4}$ mi. to S	-	357
3 mi. E of Hayfield	Upper Booth, Edale, $1\frac{3}{4}$ mi. to SSE	207	329

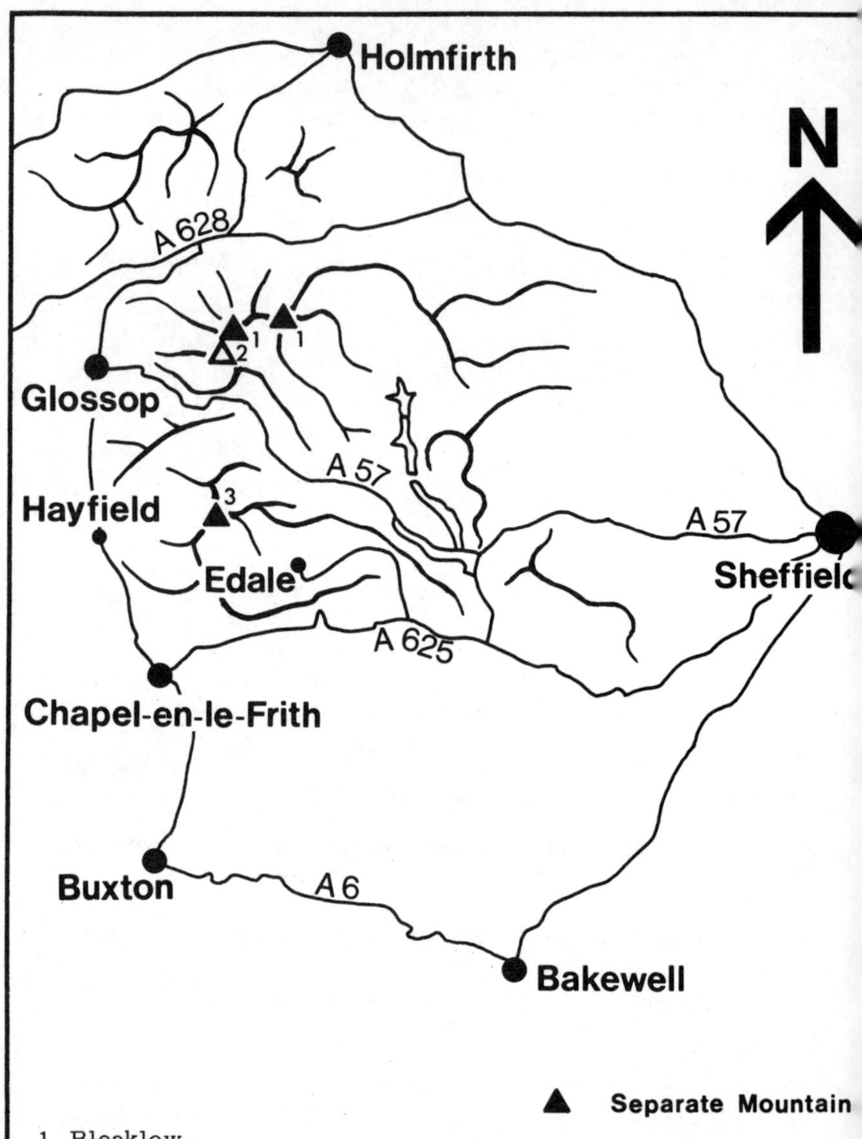

Holmfirth
N
A 628
Glossop
2
1
1
A 57
Hayfield
A 57
3
Edale
Sheffield
A 625
Chapel-en-le-Frith
Buxton
A 6
Bakewell
Separate Mountain
Subsidiary Mountain
1 Bleaklow
2 Higher Shelf Stones
3 Kinder Scout
PEAK DISTRICT

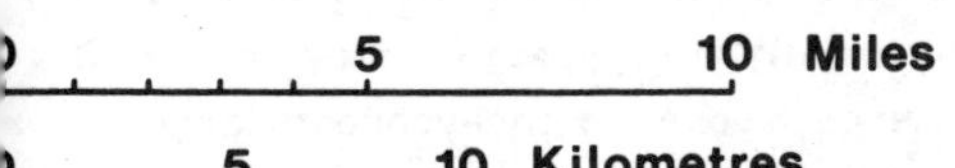

DARTMOOR
5   10 Miles
5   10 Kilometres
1   High Willhays
2   Yes Tor
Okehampton
A 30
B 3212
Tavistock
Princetown
A 384
Ashburton
Buckfastleigh
Plymouth
A 38

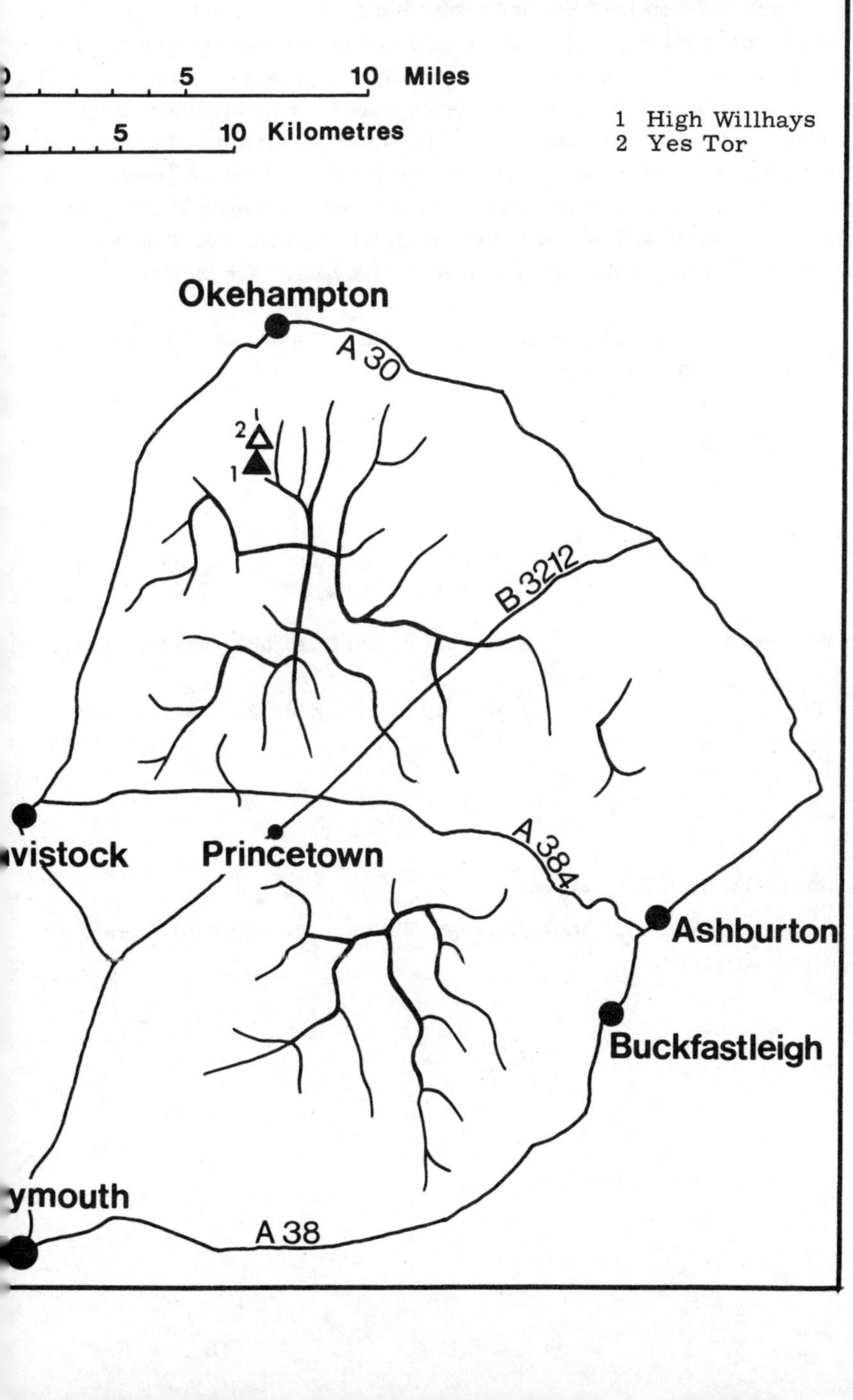

DARTMOOR

The southwestern corner of England projects out into the Atlantic in the form of a long ragged peninsula.   As a region it has strong characteristics of its own: it has at times in the past been virtually a separate country, and until about a century ago some of its people even spoke an independent language related to Welsh. But the main interest for mountaineers and hill-walkers lies in a great dome of upland country which rises athwart the peninsula in the middle of Devon. The general level of this massif is between 1500 and 2000 feet above sea level, and two summits, High Willhays and Yes Tor, manage to lift themselves above the latter height and so qualify for inclusion in this book.

The nearest towns and villages are Okehampton, Tavistock, Princetown, Buckfastleigh and Ashburton.

Name	Height		Maps			Grid	County
	feet	metres	1"	2½"	T[1]	Ref.	
High Willhays[2]	2038	621	175	SX48/58	T	579891	Devon
Yes Tor	2030	619	175	SX49/59	T	581901	Devon

<u>Notes</u>

[1] Dartmoor One-inch Tourist Map

[2] Devon County Top. Also known as High Willes, according to Crossing's "Guide to Dartmoor".

		No. in order of Altitude		Date Ascended
Position	Best Ascended From	Sep. Mtn.	Top	
3½ mi. S of Okehampton	Unclassified road, 1 mi. to E	224	358	
2½ mi. S of Okehampton	New Bridge, 1 mi. to E	-	369	

ISLE OF MAN

Ellan Vannin, as the Manx language has it, is an almost entirely mountainous island, the only substantial flat land being in its extreme north. Of the two mountain groups, the most northerly possesses just one top which rises to an altitude above the 2,000-foot contour. This is Snaefell. It is one of the only two mountains in the British Isles which has a railway running to its summit. The nearest towns and villages are Laxey, Ramsey, Sulby and Ballaugh. There are frequent ferry services to the island from Liverpool and other ports on the Mainland, and a regular air service from Blackpool.

Name	Height		Maps			Grid	County
	feet	metres	1"	2½"	T	Ref.	
Snaefell[1]	2036	620		87[2]	SC38[3]	397880	(Isle of Man)

Notes

[1] Isle of Man "County" Top.

[2] The regular One-inch Map is almost a "Tourist" map in style.

[3] Enquiries about maps of 1:25 00   (2½") scale and larger scales should be addressed to the Isle of Man Government Board, Murray House, Douglas, Isle of Man.

Position	Best Ascended From	No. in order of Altitude	Date Ascended
		Sep. Mtn.	Top
3 mi. NW of Laxey	Bungalow Station, ¾ mi. to S	226	360

WALES

The country of Wales, or to give it its proper name, Cymru, is so mountainous that it is difficult to know where to start describing it and where to stop. Its only substantial low country is the island of Anglesey, and the mountains everywhere else spill over in abundance into the adjacent parts of England. Almost everywhere high mountains confine the many fine rivers and lakes into narrow valleys which in turn can be employed as useful boundaries between the major mountain massifs. One of the more important of these valleys is the Dovey-Severn trough which runs from the sea at Aberdovey to Newtown and to Welshpool on the upper Severn, and may be said to separate the mountains of the North from those of Central Wales. Farther south is the Tywi-Wye trough which runs from Llandovery to Builth Wells and Hay, and acts as a convenient northern boundary of South Wales. Wales possesses 168 mountains 2,000 feet high or more, and an uncounted number below that altitude.

NORTH WALES

The mountains north of the Dovey-Severn trough are among the finest in Wales and indeed the whole of the British Isles. Excluding Mynydd Hiraethog (the Denbigh Moors) and the Clwyd Hills, neither of which groups include any two-thousanders, the mountains of North Wales can conveniently be described in ten groups. There are 126 two-thousanders in this northern region of Wales.

THE CARNEDDAU, THE GLYDERS, THE SNOWDON GROUP, MOEL HEBOG GROUP, MOEL SIABOD GROUP.

This is the region of Snowdonia proper, despite what the title of the National Park might seem to indicate. An alternative and even better name for the mountains of these five groups would be the old Welsh word Eryri.
The mountains of Eryri are among the best-loved British mountains of all; they hold a place in the regard of mountaineers second only to that held by those of the Lake District, with which they are in many respects directly

comparable. However, many of the mountains here are supreme in their own
right. For one thing, the seven highest peaks in England and Wales together
are in this region. Moreover, these mountains possess some of the wildest
and most dramatic - if not perhaps the most beautiful - scenery in the British
Isles. It would be hard, for instance, to find in these islands another mountain
as impressively precipitous as Tryfan. The highest mountain in Eryri, and the
acknowledged king of them all, is Snowdon itself; and even the indignity of
being one of the only two British mountains to possess a railway service to
its summit merely testifies to the immensely powerful hold it has over the
affections of visitors.

The pattern of the five mountain ranges in Eryri is comparatively simple, the
groups being demarcated by well-defined valleys which in addition carry excellent roads. The principal towns and villages include Llanberis, Beddgelert,
Rhyd-Ddu, Capel Curig, Betws-y-Coed, Bethesda, Dolwyddelan and Blaenau
Ffestiniog. The larger towns of Bangor and Caernarvon are not much farther
away.

Snowdon from Llyn Llydaw

0 1 2 3 4 5
Miles
0 5
Kilometres
Bangor
A5
Bethesda
CARNEDDAU
Llanberis
A 4086
GLYDERS
A 5
Capel Curig
Separate Mountain
Subsidiary Mountain

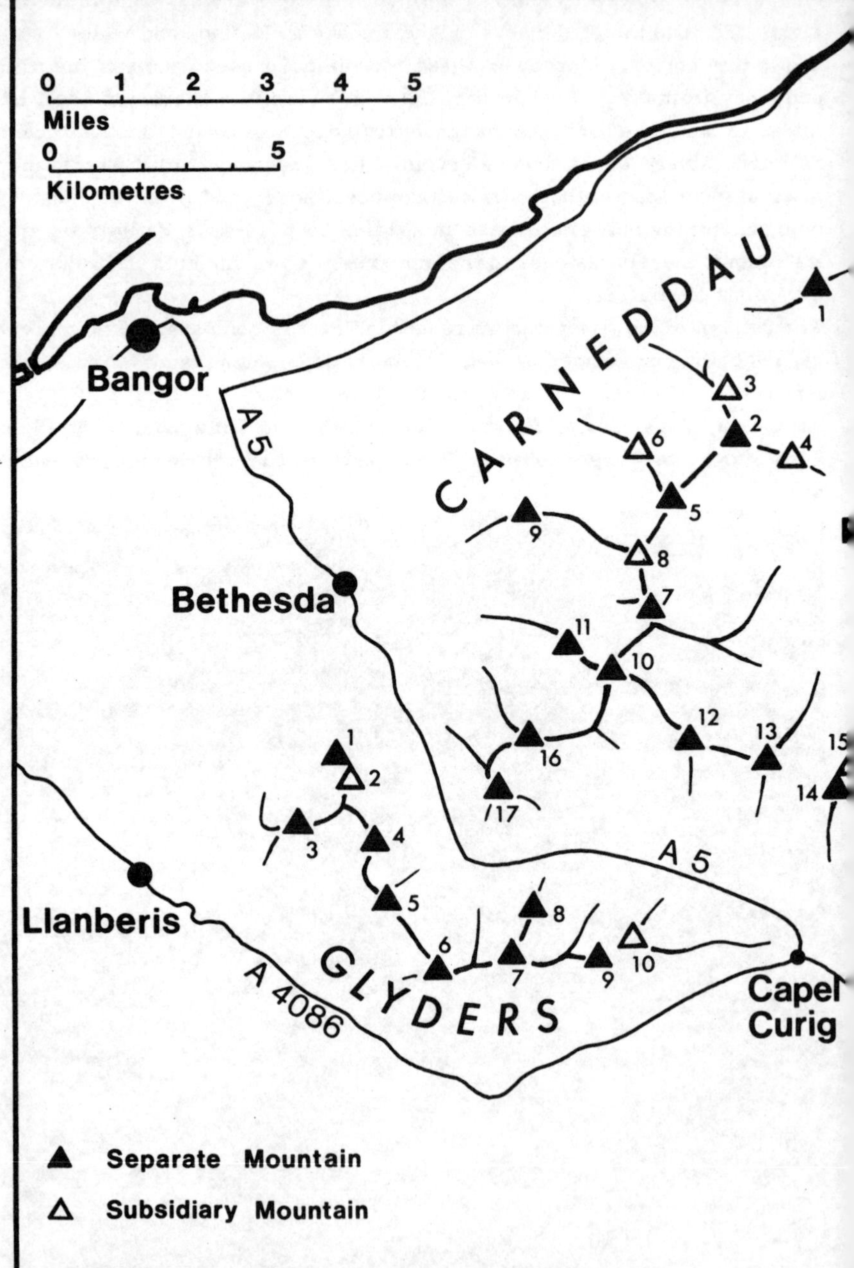

NORTH WALES:

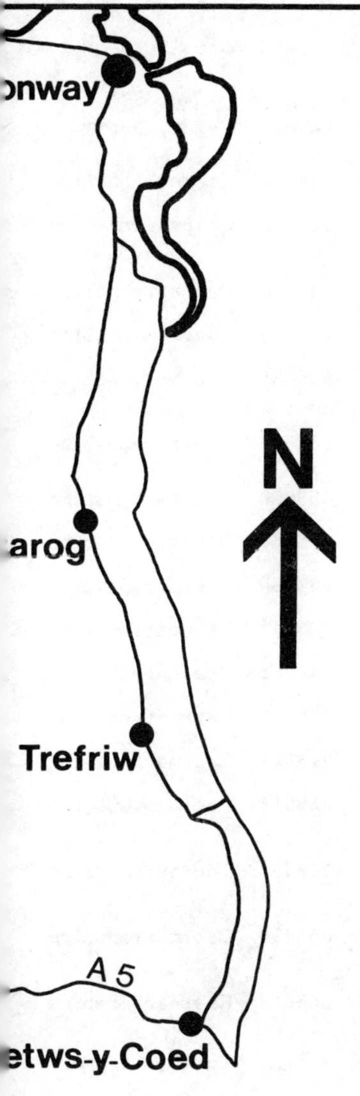

THE CARNEDDAU

1 Tal y Fan
2 Drum
3 Carnedd y Ddelw
4 Pen y Castell
5 Foel-fras
6 Llwtmor
7 Foel-grach
8 Garnedd-uchaf
9 Drosgl
10 Carnedd Llywelyn
11 Yr Elen
12 Pen yr Helgi-du
13 Pen Llithrig y Wrâch
14 Creigiau Gleision
15 Pen Cowlyd
16 Carnedd Dafydd
17 Pen-yr-oleu-wen

THE GLYDERS

1 Carnedd y Filiast
2 Mynydd Perfedd
3 Elidir Fawr
4 Foel-goch
5 Y Garn
6 Glyder Fawr
7 Glyder Fâch
8 Tryfan
9 Moel Nant yr Ogof
10 Gallt yr Ogof

THE CARNEDDAU
THE GLYDERS

THE CARNEDDAU

Name	Height		Maps			Grid	County
	feet	metres	1"	2½"	T[1]	Ref.	
Tal y Fan	2001	610	107	SH77	T	729726	Caernarvonshire
Drum (<u>summit</u> = Carnedd Penydorth-goch)[2]	2529	771	107	SH76	T	708696	Caernarvonshire
Carnedd y Ddelw	2275+	693+	107	SH77	T	708705	Caernarvonshire
Pen y Castell	2035	620	107	SH76	T	724689	Caernarvonshire
Foel-fras	3092	942	107	SH66	T	696681	Caernarvonshire
Llwytmor[3]	2750+	838+	107	SH66	T	686692	Caernarvonshire
Foel-grach	3196	974	107	SH66	T	688658	Caernarvonshire
Garnedd-uchaf	c.2980[4]	c.908	107	SH66	T	686668	Caernarvonshire
Drosgl	2484	757	107	SH66	T	663680	Caernarvonshire
Carnedd Llywelyn	3485	1062	107	SH66	T	683643	Caernarvonshire
Yr Elen	3152	961	107	SH66	T	672651	Caernarvonshire
Pen yr Helgi-du	2733	833	107	SH66	T	697630	Caernarvonshire
Pen Llithrig y Wrâch	2622	799	107	SH76	T	716622	Caernarvonshire
Creigiau Gleision	2213	675	107	SH76	T	729614	Caernarvonshire
Pen y Cowlyd[5]	2000+	610+	107	SH76	T	733622	Caernarvonshire
Carnedd Dafydd	3424	1044	107	SH66	T	662630	Caernarvonshire
Pen-yr-oleu-wen[7]	3211	979	107	SH66	T	655619	Caernarvonshire

<u>Notes</u>

[1] All the summits are in the area shown on the Snowdonia National Park Half-inch Tourist Map.

[2] Also = "Drosgl" in E. Moss's list.

[3] Also = "Llwdmor" in Rooke Corbett's list of 1929, and E. Moss's of 1940.

[4] Estimated altitude. If the contours shown on the 1:25000 (2½") map are to be relied on, the summit, whose profile is slightly pointed, could be as much as ten or twenty feet higher than this.

Position	Best Ascended From	No. in order of Altitude		Date Ascended
		Sep. Mtn.	Top	
$4\frac{1}{4}$ mi. SW of Conway	Roewen, $1\frac{3}{4}$ mi. to ESE	244	396	
4 mi. WNW of Dolgarrog	Cae-coch, 2 mi. to NE	78	118	
$4\frac{1}{4}$ mi. WNW of Dolgarrog	Cae-coch, $1\frac{1}{2}$ mi. to ENE	-	213	
3 mi. WNW of Dolgarrog	Cae-coch, $1\frac{3}{4}$ mi. to NNE	-	364	
$4\frac{1}{2}$ mi. W of Dolgarrog	Llanbedr-y-cennin, 4 mi. to ENE	14	14	
4 mi. NE of Bethesda	Unclassified road, $1\frac{1}{2}$ mi. to NNW	-	62	
5 mi. WSW of Dolgarrog	Gerlan, $3\frac{1}{2}$ mi. to W	9	9	
4 mi. E of Bethesda	Gerlan, 3 mi. to W	-	23	
$2\frac{1}{2}$ mi. ENE of Bethesda	Gerlan, $2\frac{1}{4}$ mi. to WNW	86	132	
$3\frac{3}{4}$ mi. ESE of Bethesda	Gerlan, $3\frac{1}{4}$ mi. to WNW	3	3	
3 mi. ESE of Bethesda	Gerlan, $2\frac{1}{2}$ mi. to WNW	11	11	
$3\frac{1}{4}$ mi. NNW of Capel Curig	Helyg, $1\frac{3}{4}$ mi. to SSW	46	65	
$2\frac{1}{2}$ mi. N of Capel Curig	Tal-y-waen, 2 mi. to S	63	91	
2 mi. NNE of Capel Curig	Unclassified road, 1 mi. to SE	160	248	
$2\frac{1}{2}$ mi. NNW of Capel Curig	Unclassified road, $1\frac{1}{2}$ mi. to E	-	404	
3 mi. SE of Bethesda	Tal-y-llyn Ogwen, $1\frac{1}{2}$ mi. to S	4	4	
$3\frac{1}{2}$ mi. SSE of Bethesda	Pont Pen-y-benglog, 1 mi. to SSW	7	7	

[5] Author's temporary name, from Llyn Cowlyd to the west.

[7] Spelling according to general usage. On O.S. Maps "Penyrole-wen."

THE GLYDERS

Name	Height feet	Metres	Maps 1"	2½" T[1]	Grid Ref.	County
Carnedd y Filiast	2695	821	107	SH66 T	620627	Caernarvonshire
Mynydd Perfedd	2665	812	107	SH66 T	622618	Caernarvonshire
Elidir Fawr	3030	924	107	SH66 T	612613	Caernarvonshire
Foel-goch	2727	831	107	SH66 T	628612	Caernarvonshire
Y Garn	3104	946	107	SH65 T	630595	Caernarvonshire
Glyder Fawr	3279	999	107	SH65 T	642579	Caernarvonshire
Glyder Fâch (<u>summit</u> = <u>Gwyliwr</u>)	3262	994	107	SH65 T	656582	Caernarvonshire
Tryfan	3010	917	107	SH65 T	663594	Caernarvonshire
Moel Nant yr Ogof[2]	2642[3]	805	107	SH65 T	677581	Caernarvonshire
Gallt yr Ogof	2499	762	107	SH65 T	685585	Caernarvonshire

<u>Notes</u>

[1] All the summits are in the area shown on the Snowdonia National Park Half-inch Tourist Map.

[2] Author's temporary name, from small valley, Nant yr Ogof, to the N.

[3] Six-inch Map. Points 2642 and 2636 are Spot Heights about 80 yards apart, on and near the summit. The 2650-foot contour ring shown on the 2½" map should be treated with reservations.

Position	Best Ascended From	No. in order of Altitude		Date Ascended
		Sep. Mtn.	Top	
$2\frac{1}{2}$ mi. S of Bethesda	Maescaradog, 1 mi. to E	52	75	
3 mi. S of Bethesda	Maescaradog, 1 mi. to NE	-	79	
$2\frac{1}{4}$ mi. ENE of Llanberis	Pentre, $1\frac{3}{4}$ mi. to E	16	18	
$3\frac{1}{4}$ mi. S of Bethesda	Pentre, $\frac{3}{4}$ mi. to ENE	47	67	
$4\frac{1}{4}$ mi. S of Bethesda	Ogwen Cottage, $1\frac{1}{4}$ mi. to ENE	13	13	
$5\frac{1}{2}$ mi. SSE of Bethesda	Ogwen Cottage, $1\frac{1}{2}$ mi. to ENE	5	5	
$5\frac{1}{2}$ mi. SSE of Bethesda	Ogwen Cottage, $1\frac{1}{2}$ mi. to NNW	6	6	
$3\frac{1}{2}$ mi. W of Capel Curig	Gwern-gof-uchaf, $\frac{3}{4}$ mi. to NE	18	21	
$2\frac{3}{4}$ mi. W of Capel Curig	Gwern-gof-isaf, (685600), $1\frac{1}{4}$ mi. to NNE	57	84	
$2\frac{1}{4}$ mi. W of Capel Curig	Gwern-gof-isaf, (685600), 1 mi. to N	-	129	

Caernarvon
Llanberis
SNOWDON GROUP
HEBOG
Nantlle
Rhyd-ddu
Beddgelert
MOEL SIARO
GROUP
Tremadoc
Portmadoc
0 1 2 3 4 5
Miles
N
Separate Mountain
Subsidiary Mo

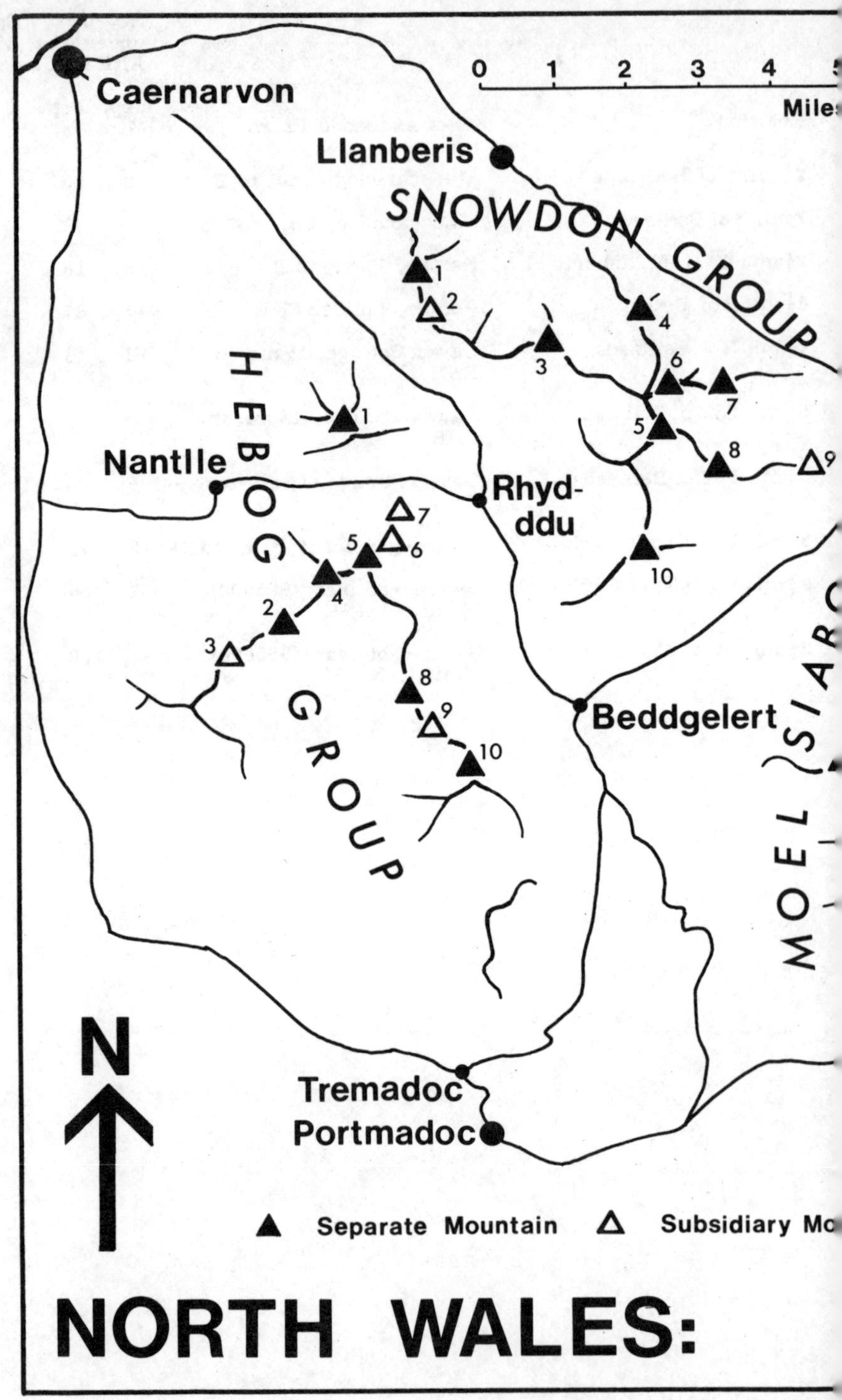

NORTH WALES:

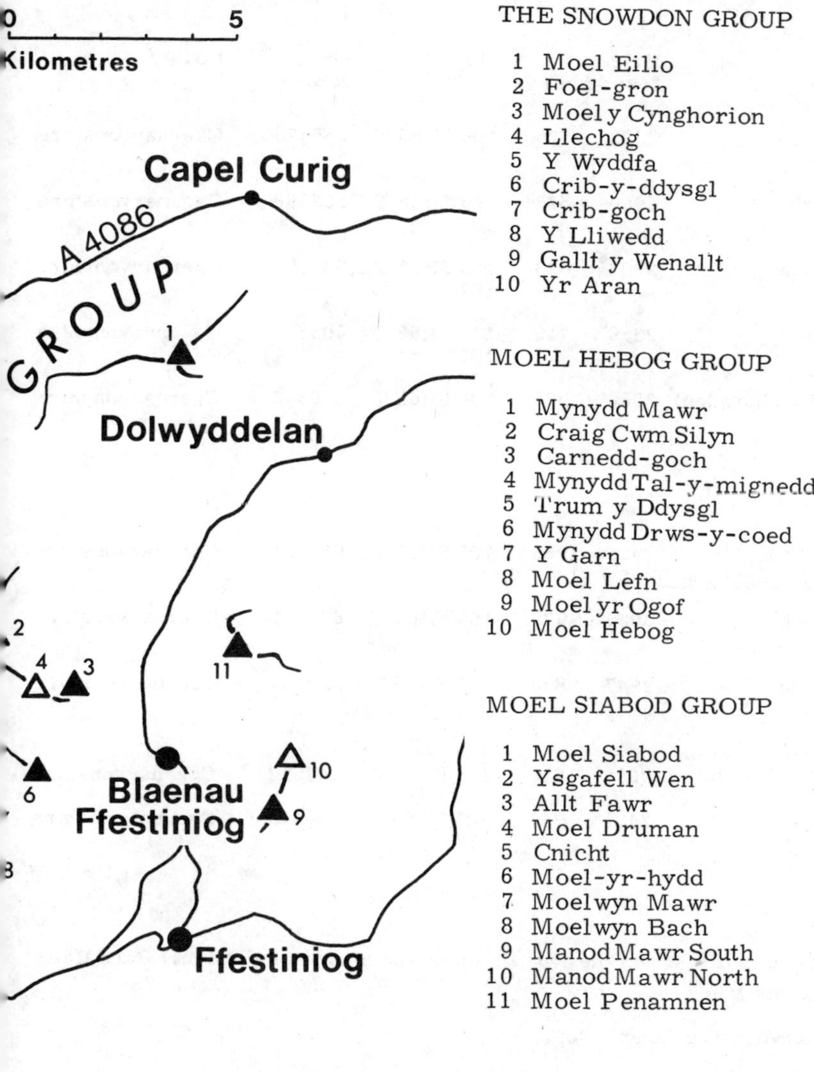

THE SNOWDON GROUP

1 Moel Eilio
2 Foel-gron
3 Moel y Cynghorion
4 Llechog
5 Y Wyddfa
6 Crib-y-ddysgl
7 Crib-goch
8 Y Lliwedd
9 Gallt y Wenallt
10 Yr Aran

MOEL HEBOG GROUP

1 Mynydd Mawr
2 Craig Cwm Silyn
3 Carnedd-goch
4 Mynydd Tal-y-mignedd
5 Trum y Ddysgl
6 Mynydd Drws-y-coed
7 Y Garn
8 Moel Lefn
9 Moel yr Ogof
10 Moel Hebog

MOEL SIABOD GROUP

1 Moel Siabod
2 Ysgafell Wen
3 Allt Fawr
4 Moel Druman
5 Cnicht
6 Moel-yr-hydd
7 Moelwyn Mawr
8 Moelwyn Bach
9 Manod Mawr South
10 Manod Mawr North
11 Moel Penamnen

SNOWDON GROUP
MOEL HEBOG GROUP
MOEL SIABOD GROUP

SNOWDON GROUP

Name	Height		Maps	Grid	County
	feet	metres	1" 2½" T[1]	Ref.	
Moel Eilio	2382	726	106 SH55 T 107	555576	Caernarvonshire
Foel-gron	2050+	625+	106 SH55 T 107	559568	Caernarvonshire
Moel y Cynghorion	2207[6]	673	106 SH55 T 107	c.585563	Caernarvonshire
Llechog	2359[6]	719	106 SH65 T 107	605567	Caernarvonshire
Y Wyddfa (Snowdon)[2]	3560	1085	106 SH65 T 107	609543	Caernarvonshire
Crib-y-ddysgl[3] (summit = Carnedd Ugain)	3496	1066	107 SH65 T	610551	Caernarvonshire
Crib-goch[4]	3026[5]	922	107 SH65 T	624551	Caernarvonshire
Y Lliwedd	2947	898	107 SH65 T	622533	Caernarvonshire
Gallt y Wenallt	2032	619	107 SH65 T	642532	Caernarvonshire
Yr Aran	2451	747	107 SH65 T 116	604515	Caernarvonshire

Notes

[1] All the summits are in the area shown on the Snowdonia National Park Half-inch Tourist Map.

[2] Caernarvonshire County Top.

[3] Also: (Y) Grib Ddesgil (locally).

[4] (Y) "Grib-goch" on O.S. maps.

[5] Six-inch Map. Point 3026 is at the middle of the ridge. Point 3023, the only height given on the 1:25000 (2½") map and those of smaller scales, is at the eastern end, at 626552.

[6] Six-inch Map.

| | | No. in order of Altitude | | Date Asc-ended |
Position	Best Ascended From	Sep. Mtn.	Top	
2 mi. SW of Llanberis	Snowdon Ranger, $1\frac{3}{4}$ mi. to SSE	107	164	
$2\frac{1}{2}$ mi. SSW of Llanberis	Snowdon Ranger $1\frac{1}{4}$ mi. to SSE	-	348	
$2\frac{1}{2}$ mi. SSE of Llanberis	Snowdon Ranger $1\frac{1}{2}$ mi. to SW	165	254	
3 mi. SE of Llanberis	A. 4086 road near Ynys Ettws, 1 mi. to E	115	175	
4 mi. SE of Llanberis	Pen-y-pass (Gorphwysfa), $2\frac{1}{2}$ mi. to ENE; Nantgwynant, $2\frac{1}{2}$ mi. to SSE; Pitt's Head, $2\frac{3}{4}$ mi. to SW; Llanberis, $4\frac{1}{4}$ mi. to NNW	1	1	
$3\frac{3}{4}$ mi. SE of Llanberis	Pen-y-pass (Gorphwysfa), $2\frac{1}{4}$ mi. to E	2	2	
$4\frac{1}{4}$ mi. SE of Llanberis	Pen-y-pass (Gorphwysfa), $1\frac{1}{4}$ mi. to E	17	19	
$3\frac{3}{4}$ mi. NNE of Beddgelert	Pen-y-pass (Gorphwysfa), 2 mi. to NE; Nantgwynant, $1\frac{3}{4}$ mi. to S	23	28	
$4\frac{1}{2}$ mi. NE of Beddgelert	A. 498 road, $1\frac{1}{4}$ mi. to NE	-	366	
$2\frac{1}{4}$ mi. NNE of Beddgelert	Nantgwynant, $1\frac{1}{2}$ mi. to ESE	96	143	

MOEL HEBOG GROUP

Name	Height feet	metres	Maps 1" 2½" T[1]		Grid Ref.	County
Mynydd Mawr	2290	698	106 107	SH55 T	539546	Caernarvonshire
Craig Cwm Silyn	2408	734	107 116	SH55 T	525502	Caernarvonshire
Garnedd-goch	2302	702	107 116	SH55 T	511495	Caernarvonshire
Mynydd Tal-y-mignedd	2148	655	107 116	SH55 T	535514	Caernarvonshire
Trum y Ddysgl	2329	710	107 116	SH55 T	544516	Caernarvonshire
Mynydd Drws-y-coed	2286[6]	697	107 116	SH55 T	548518	Caernarvonshire
Y Garn	2080	634	107 116	SH55 T	551526	Caernarvonshire
Moel Lefn	2094	638	107 116	SH54 T	553485	Caernarvonshire
Moel yr Ogof	2000+	610+	107 116	SH54 T	c.555477	Caernarvonshire
Moel Hebog	2568	783	107 116	SH54 T	564469	Caernarvonshire

Notes

[1] All the summits are in the area shown on the Snowdonia National Park Half-inch Tourist Map.

[2] For many years there have been difficulties of access to some of these mountains. The present position appears to be that access is forbidden along the NW, SW and S approaches of Mynydd Mawr, and along the N and NW approaches of Y Garn and Mynydd Drws-y-coed. Visitors are asked to avoid these approaches so as not to prejudice the National Park authorities' negotiations for access.

[6] Six-inch Map.

Position	Best Ascended From[2]	No. in order of Altitude		Date Asc-ended
		Sep. Mtn.	Top	
5 mi. NW of Beddgelert	Nantlle, 2 mi. to WSW	138	206	
4 mi. WNW of Beddgelert	Cwm Trwsgl, 1 mi. to SE; Tan-yr-allt, $2\frac{1}{2}$ mi. to NNW	105	157	
5 mi. WNW of Beddgelert	Cwm Trwsgl, $1\frac{3}{4}$ mi. to E; Tan-yr-allt, 2 mi. to NNW	-	201	
4 mi. NW of Beddgelert	Cwm Trwsgl, $1\frac{1}{2}$ mi. to S; Tan-yr-allt, 3 mi. to W	192	299	
$3\frac{1}{2}$ mi. NW of Beddgelert	Cwm Trwsgl, $1\frac{1}{2}$ mi. to SSW; Tan-yr-allt, $3\frac{1}{2}$ mi. to W	125	188	
$3\frac{1}{2}$ mi. NW of Beddgelert	Cwm Trwsgl, $1\frac{3}{4}$ mi. to SSW; Tan-yr-allt, $3\frac{3}{4}$ mi. to W	-	210	
$3\frac{3}{4}$ mi. NW of Beddgelert	Cwm Trwsgl, $2\frac{1}{4}$ mi. to SSW; Tan-yr-allt, 4 mi. to W		331	
$2\frac{1}{4}$ mi. W of Beddgelert	Cwm Trwsgl, 1 mi. to W; Beddgelert, $2\frac{1}{4}$ mi. to E	205	325	
2 mi. W of Beddgelert	Beddgelert, 2 mi. to E	-	403	
$1\frac{3}{4}$ mi. SW of Beddgelert	Beddgelert, $1\frac{3}{4}$ mi. to NE	71	108	

MOEL SIABOD GROUP

Name	Height feet	metres	Maps 1" 2½" T^1	Grid Ref.	County
Moel Siabod (summit = Carnedd Moel Siabod)	2861	872	107 SH75 T	705546	Caernarvonshire
Ysgafell Wen[2]	2192	668	107 SH64 T 116	663485	Caernarvonshire
Allt Fawr	2287	697	107 SH64 T 116	681474	Caernarvonshire and Merionethshire
Moel Druman	2152	656	107 SH64 T 116	669475	Merionethshire
Cnicht	2265	690	107 SH64 T 116	645566	Caernarvonshire and Merionethshire
Moel-yr-hydd	2124	647	107 SH64 T 116	672454	Merionethshire
Moelwyn Mawr	2527	770	107 SH64 T 116	658448	Merionethshire
Moelwyn Bach	2334	711	107 SH64 T 116	660437	Merionethshire
Manod Mawr South[3]	2167	661	107 SH74 T 116	724446	Merionethshire
Manod Mawr North[4]	2158	658	107 SH74 T 116	727458	Merionethshire
Moel Penamnen	2000+	610+	107 SH74 T 116	c.716483	Caernarvonshire and Merionethshire

Notes

[1] All the summits are in the area shown on the Snowdonia National Park Half-inch Tourist Map.

[2] Also ="Moel Bleiddiau" in Docharty's list.

[3] Appears as Clogwyn Candryll in E. Moss's list.

[4] Appears as Graig-ddu in E. Moss's list.

Position	Best Ascended From	No. in order of Altitude		Date Ascended
		Sep. Mtn.	Top	
$2\frac{1}{4}$ mi. NW of Dolwyddelan	Dolwyddelan, $2\frac{1}{4}$ mi. to SE; Pont Cyfyng, Capel Curig, $2\frac{1}{4}$ mi. NE	33	41	
$2\frac{3}{4}$ mi. NW of Blaenau Ffestiniog	Tanygrisiau, $2\frac{1}{2}$ mi. to SSE	172	267	
$1\frac{1}{2}$ mi. NW of Blaenau Ffestiniog	Tanygrisiau, $1\frac{1}{2}$ mi. to SSE	139	208	
$2\frac{1}{4}$ mi. NW of Blaenau Ffestiniog	Tanygrisiau, $1\frac{3}{4}$ mi. to SSE	-	294	
$3\frac{1}{2}$ mi. W of Blaenau Ffestiniog	Croesor, $1\frac{1}{2}$ mi. to SW	143	217	
2 mi. W of Blaenau Ffestiniog	Tanygrisiau, 1 mi. to ESE	198	312	
$2\frac{3}{4}$ mi. W of Blaenau Ffestiniog	Tanygrisiau, $1\frac{3}{4}$ mi. to E	79	119	
3 mi. WSW of Blaenau Ffestiniog	Tanygrisiau, $1\frac{3}{4}$ mi. to ENE	120	183	
$1\frac{1}{2}$ mi. SE of Blaenau Ffestiniog	Blaenau Ffestiniog, $1\frac{1}{2}$ mi. to NW	183	281	
$1\frac{1}{2}$ mi. E of Blaenau Ffestiniog	Blaenau Ffestiniog, $1\frac{1}{2}$ mi. to W	-	289	
$1\frac{3}{4}$ mi. NE of Blaenau Ffestiniog	Blaenau Ffestiniog, $1\frac{3}{4}$ mi. to SW	247	402	

Lliwedd, Snowdon, Crib-y-ddysgl and Crib-goch

THE ARENNIGS, BERWYNS, ARANS, RHINOGS, CADER IDRIS

This region of five grand mountain groups is together sometimes known, use-
fully but not too accurately, as Merion.   Its structure as a region is even
simpler than that of Eryri; here too, several important valleys separate the
main mountain massifs; and the Arans, Berwyns and Cader Idris range form
part of a long and complicated ridge which extends from the gorge of the River
Dee at Llangollen to the sea between Barmouth and Aberdovey. (The Clwyd
Hills can be thought of as a less elevated northern extension of this ridge.)
The Rhinogs and Cader Idris share with the mountains of Eryri the same wild
rugged characteristics, and Cader in particular lies second to none in sheer
dramatic impact.

The nearest towns and villages include Dolgellau, Bala, Dinas Mawddwy,
Llanuwchllyn and Machynlleth.

Cader Idris from the North

Pentrefoelas
A 5
Ffestiniog
Ll. Celyn
ARENNIGS
Bala
Traws-
fynydd
BER
A 494
ARANS
L. Vyrnwy
Dolgellau
Dinas Mawddwy
A 458
0   5   10   Miles
0   5   10   Kilometres

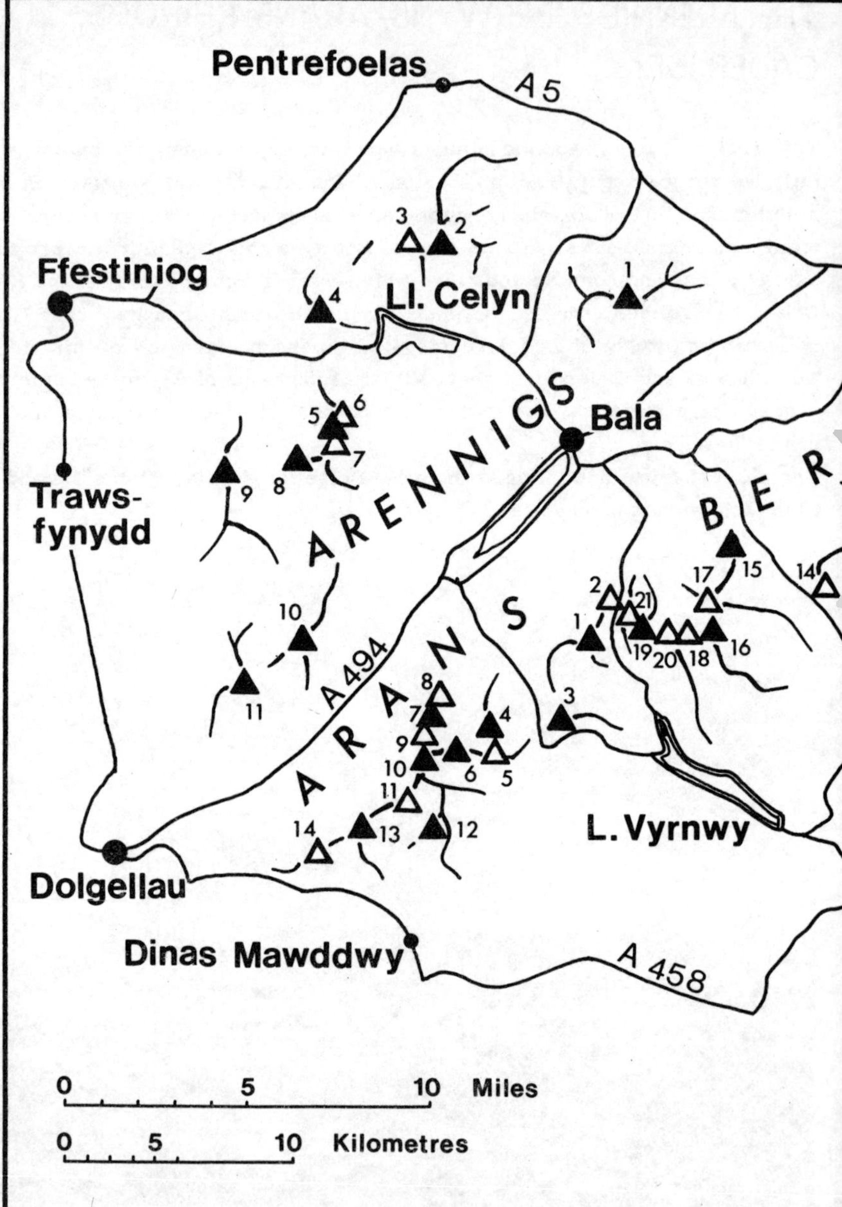

NORTH WALES:

THE ARENNIGS
THE BERWYNS
THE ARANS

THE ARENNIGS

Name	Height		Maps			Grid	County
	feet	metres	1"	2½"	T[1]	Ref.	
Foel Goch	2004	611	108	SH94	T	953422	Denbighshire and
			117				Merionethshire
Gylchedd (<u>summit</u> = <u>Carnedd y Filiast</u>)	2195	669	107	SH84	T	871445	Denbighshire and
			116				Merionethshire
Carnedd Llechwedd[2]	2109[6]	643	107	SH84	T	857446	Denbighshire and
			116				Merionethshire
Arennig Fach (<u>summit</u> = <u>Carnedd Bochgen</u>)	2259	689	107	SH84	T	820415	Merionethshire
			116				
Arennig Fawr (<u>summit</u> = <u>Moel yr Eglwys</u>[3])	2801[9]	854	116	SH83	T	826369	Merionethshire
Moel Llechwedd[4]	2700+	823+	116	SH83	T	829372	Merionethshire
Pen y Diocyn[5]	2731	832	116	SH83	T	826366	Merionethshire
Moel Llyfnant	2461	750	116	SH83	T	808351	Merionethshire
Foel Boeth[7]	2021	616	116	SH73	T	778344	Merionethshire
Y Dduallt[8]	2155	657	116	SH82	T	810273	Merionethshire
Rhobell Fawr	2409[9]	734	116	SH72	T	786256	Merionethshire

<u>Notes</u>

[1] All the summits are in the area shown on the Snowdonia National Park Half-inch Tourist Map.

[2] From the Six-inch Map.   Also = "Point SE" of E. Moss's list.

[3] Summit name from Six-inch Map. "S Top" in E. Moss's list.

[4] Author's temporary name.

[5] Author's temporary name; from Carreg y Diocyn, ½ mile to E.

[6] Six-inch Map.

[7] Twin summits, the SSE and lower (2000+ feet) one having the summit name Gallt y Daren (Six-inch Map).

[8] Source of the Afon Dyfrdwy, known as the River Dee in England; reaches the sea near Chester.

[9] Half-inch Tourist Map.

Position	Best Ascended From	No. in order of Altitude		Date Ascended
		Sep. Mtn.	Top	
4 mi. NNE of Bala town	Llangwm, $1\frac{3}{4}$ mi. to NE	238	388	
$2\frac{1}{2}$ mi. N of Llyn Celyn	Blaen-y-cwm, 2 mi. to ENE; Llyn Celyn, $2\frac{1}{2}$ mi. to S	171	266	
$2\frac{1}{2}$ mi. N of Llyn Celyn	Blaen-y-cwm, $2\frac{3}{4}$ mi. to ENE; Llyn Celyn, $2\frac{1}{2}$ mi. to S	-	316	
$1\frac{1}{2}$ mi. W of Llyn Celyn	Nant-yr-helfa, 1 mi. to SSE	147	221	
$2\frac{1}{4}$ mi. SW of Llyn Celyn	Nant-yr-helfa, 2 mi. to N	39	52	
2 mi. SW of Llyn Celyn	Nant-yr-helfa, $1\frac{3}{4}$ mi. to N	-	73	
$2\frac{1}{2}$ mi. SW of Llyn Celyn	Nant-yr-helfa, 2 mi. to N	-	66	
4 mi. SW of Llyn Celyn	Nant ddu, 2 mi. to N	93	140	
4 mi. E of Trawsfynydd village	Dol-haidd, 2 mi. to NW	231	376	
8 mi. NE of Dolgellau	Caer-dynyn, 2 mi. to SE	188	291	
6 mi. NE of Dolgellau	Nannau-is-afan, 2 mi. to W	104	156	

THE BERWYNS

Name	Height		Maps	Grid	County
	feet	metres	1" 2½" T	Ref.	
Moel Fferna	2071	631	117 SJ13	116397	Merionethshire
Cadair Bronwen (<u>summit = Bwrdd Arthur</u>)	2572	784	117 SJ03	077346	Denbighshire and Merionethshire
Pen-y-bryn[1]	2250+	686+	117 SJ03	086352	Denbighshire and Merionethshire
Y Foel[1]	2028[6]	618	117 SJ03	089368	Merionethshire
Moel Sych[2]	2713	827	117 SJ03	066318	Denbighshire, Merionethshire and Montgomeryshire
Cadair Berwyn	2712	827	117 SJ03	072327	Denbighshire and Merionethshire
Tomle	2431	741	117 SJ03	085335	Denbighshire
Foel Wen	2265	690	117 SJ03	099333	Denbighshire
Mynydd Tarw	2230	680	117 SJ13	112324	Denbighshire
Rhos	2030	619	117 SJ13	124323	Denbighshire
Godor	2226	678	117 SJ03	094307	Denbighshire
Moel Poethion[3]	2239	682	117 SJ03	082306	Denbighshire
Post Gwyn	2150+	655+	117 SJ02	048293	Montgomeryshire
Bryn-gwyn[1]	2025+	617+	117 SJ02	042295	Montgomeryshire
Trum y Sarn[4]	2127	648	117 SH93 T[7]	995313	Merionethshire
Cyrniau Nôd	2185	666	117 SH92 T[7]	988278	Merionethshire and Montgomeryshire
Y Groes Fagl[6]	2162	659	117 SH92 T[7]	988289	Merionethshire and Montgomeryshire
Cefn Gwyntog	2000+	610+	117 SH92 T[7]	976277	Merionethshire and Montgomeryshire
Pen y Boncyn trefeilw[5]	2150+	655+	117 SH92 T[7]	957280	Merionethshire
Stac Rhôs[6]	2100+	640+	117 SH92 T[7]	968276	Merionethshire and Montgomeryshire
Pen y Cerrig-duon[6]	2000+	610+	117 SH92 T[7]	952281	Merionethshire

Position	Best Ascended From	No. in order of Altitude		Date Asc-ended
		Sep. Mtn.	Top	
3½ mi. SE of Corwen	Plasnewydd, 1¼ mi. to NE	212	337	
5½ mi. S of Corwen	Llandrillo, 3 mi. to NW	70	106	
5 mi. S of Corwen	Llandrillo, 3½ mi. to NNW	-	228	
4 mi. S of Corwen	Llandrillo, 3½ mi. to W	-	371	
7 mi. S of Corwen	Tan-y-pistyll, 1½ mi. to SSW	49	69	
6½ mi. S of Corwen	Tan-y-pistyll, 2 mi. to S	-	70	
6 mi. S of Corwen	Blaen-y-cwm, 1 mi. to SE	-	148	
6½ mi. SSE of Corwen	Blaen-y-cwm, ¾ mi. to S	144	218	
7 mi. SSE of Corwen	Tyn-y-ffridd, 1 mi. to SE	-	239	
7½ mi. SSW of Corwen	Tyn-y-ffridd, 1 mi. to SSW	-	368	
8 mi. SSE of Corwen	Blaen-y-cwm, 1 mi. to N	156	243	
8 mi. S of Corwen	Tan-y-pistyll, 1 mi. to SW	151	234	
9 mi. SSW of Corwen	B. 4391 road, ¾ mi. to SW	191	297	
9 mi. SSW of Corwen	B. 4391 road, ½ mi. to SW	-	372	
5 mi. SE of Bala town	Pont Cwm-pydew, ¾ mi. to E	196	309	
4 mi. N of Lake Vyrnwy	Cwm Pennant, 2 mi. to SE	177	273	
4½ mi. N of Lake Vyrnwy	B. 4391 road, 2 mi. to NE	-	285	
3½ mi. N of Lake Vyrnwy	Head of L. Vyrnwy, 2¼ mi. to SSW	-	401	
2½ mi. N of Lake Vyrnwy	Head of L. Vyrnwy, 2½ mi. to S	190	296	
3 mi. N of Lake Vyrnwy	Head of L. Vyrnwy, 2¼ mi. to S	-	323	
2½ mi. NNW of Lake Vyrnwy	Head of L. Vyrnwy, 2½ mi. to SSE	-	405	

<u>Notes</u>

[1] Author's temporary name.

[2] County Top for both Denbighshire and Montgomeryshire.

[3] Author's temporary name; from Cerrig Poethion to W (Six-inch Map).

[5] Twin summits, of equal height, the other one being at 961282, a few hundred yards to the NE.

[6] Six-inch Map.

[4] Six-inch Map. "Foel Cwm-pydew" (Docharty); "Point 2127" (E. Moss).

[7] Snowdonia National Park Half-inch Tourist Map.

THE ARANS

Name	Height		Maps			Grid	County
	feet	metres	1"	2½"	T[1]	Ref.	
Foel y Geifr[2]	2055[16]	626	117	SH92	T	937375	Merionethshire
Foel Goch[3]	2000+	610+	117	SH92	T	944292	Merionethshire
Moel y Cerrig-duon	2049	625	117	SH92	T	923241	Merionethshire and Montgomeryshire
Foel Rhudd	2100+	640+	117	SH82	T	895238	Merionethshire
Llechwedd Du[4]	2010	613	117	SH82	T	893223	Merionethshire
Foel Hafod-fynydd[5]	2250+[7]	686+	116	SH82	T	877226	Merionethshire
Aran Benllyn[8]	2901	884	116	SH82	T	867242	Merionethshire
Pen-aran[9]	2775	846	116	SH82	T	868246	Merionethshire
Erw y Ddafad-ddu[10]	2838	865	116	SH82	T	865234	Merionethshire
Aran Fawddwy[11]	2974[16]	906	116	SH82	T	862223	Merionethshire
Gwaen y Llŵyni[12]	2248	685	116	SH82	T	857204	Merionethshire
Pen yr Allt-uchaf[13]	2000+	610+	116	SH81	T	870195	Merionethshire
Glasgwym[14]	2557	779	116	SH81	T	836194	Merionethshire
Pen y Bryn-fforchog[15]	2149	655	116	SH81	T	816183	Merionethshire

<u>Notes</u>

[1] All the summits are in the area shown on the Snowdonia National Park Half-inch Tourist Map.

[2] Also: Mynydd Carnedd Hywel.

[3] "Foel Hirnant" (Docharty) and "Point N (i)" (E. Moss).

[4] Six-inch Map. Also: Craig Ty-nant (Docharty and E. Moss).

[5] Six-inch Map. Also: Craig Cwm-du (Docharty and E. Moss).

[7] Contour ring to W of Spot Height 2246 on One-inch and other maps.

[8] "N Top" (E. Moss).

[9] Author's temporary name; from Llyn Pen-aran near summit (Six-inch Map). Also: "Far N Top" (E. Moss).

Position	Best Ascended From	No. in order of Altitude		Date Ascended
		Sep. Mtn.	Top	
3 mi. NW of Lake Vyrnwy	Head of Lake Vyrnwy, $2\frac{1}{2}$ mi. to SE	218	345	
$3\frac{1}{2}$ mi. NNW of Lake Vyrnwy	Head of Lake Vyrnwy, $3\frac{1}{2}$ mi. to SSE	-	398	
3 mi. NW of Lake Vyrnwy	Waun y Gadfa, $\frac{1}{2}$ mi. to S	220	350	
$4\frac{1}{2}$ mi. WNW of Lake Vyrnwy	Tan-y-bwlch, 1 mi. to ENE	202	320	
$4\frac{1}{2}$ mi. W of Lake Vyrnwy	Blaen-pennant, 1 mi. to SE	-	383	
5 mi. NNE of Dinas Mawddwy	Blaen-pennant, 2 mi. to SE	148	226	
$3\frac{1}{2}$ mi. S of Llanuwchllyn	Pant-clyd, $1\frac{3}{4}$ mi. to NW	30	36	
$3\frac{1}{4}$ mi. S of Llanuwchllyn	Pant-clyd, $1\frac{3}{4}$ mi. to NW	-	55	
4 mi. S of Llanuwchllyn	Pant-clyd, 2 mi. to NW	-	43	
$4\frac{1}{2}$ mi. N of Dinas Mawddwy	Pant-clyd, $2\frac{1}{4}$ mi. to NW	20	24	
$3\frac{1}{2}$ mi. N of Dinas Mawddwy	Cwm Cowarch, 1 mi. to SSW	-	232	
3 mi. NE of Dinas Mawddwy	Cwm Cowarch, 1 mi. to SW	248	406	
3 mi. NNW of Dinas Mawddwy	Cwm Cowarch, 1 mi. to SE	73	110	
$3\frac{1}{2}$ mi. NW of Dinas Mawddwy	Pont Buarth-glas, $1\frac{1}{4}$ mi. to SSE	-	298	

[10]Six-inch Map. Also: "S Top" (E. Moss).

[11]Merionethshire County Top.

[12]Six-inch Map. Also: "Camddwr" (E. Moss).

[13]Six-inch Map. ? Also: "Drysgol, Point S" (E. Moss).

[14]Also: "Craig y Ffynon" (Rooke Corbett 1911 and 1929, and E. Moss).

[15]Six-inch Map. Also: "Point 2149" (E. Moss).

[16]Half-inch Tourist Map.

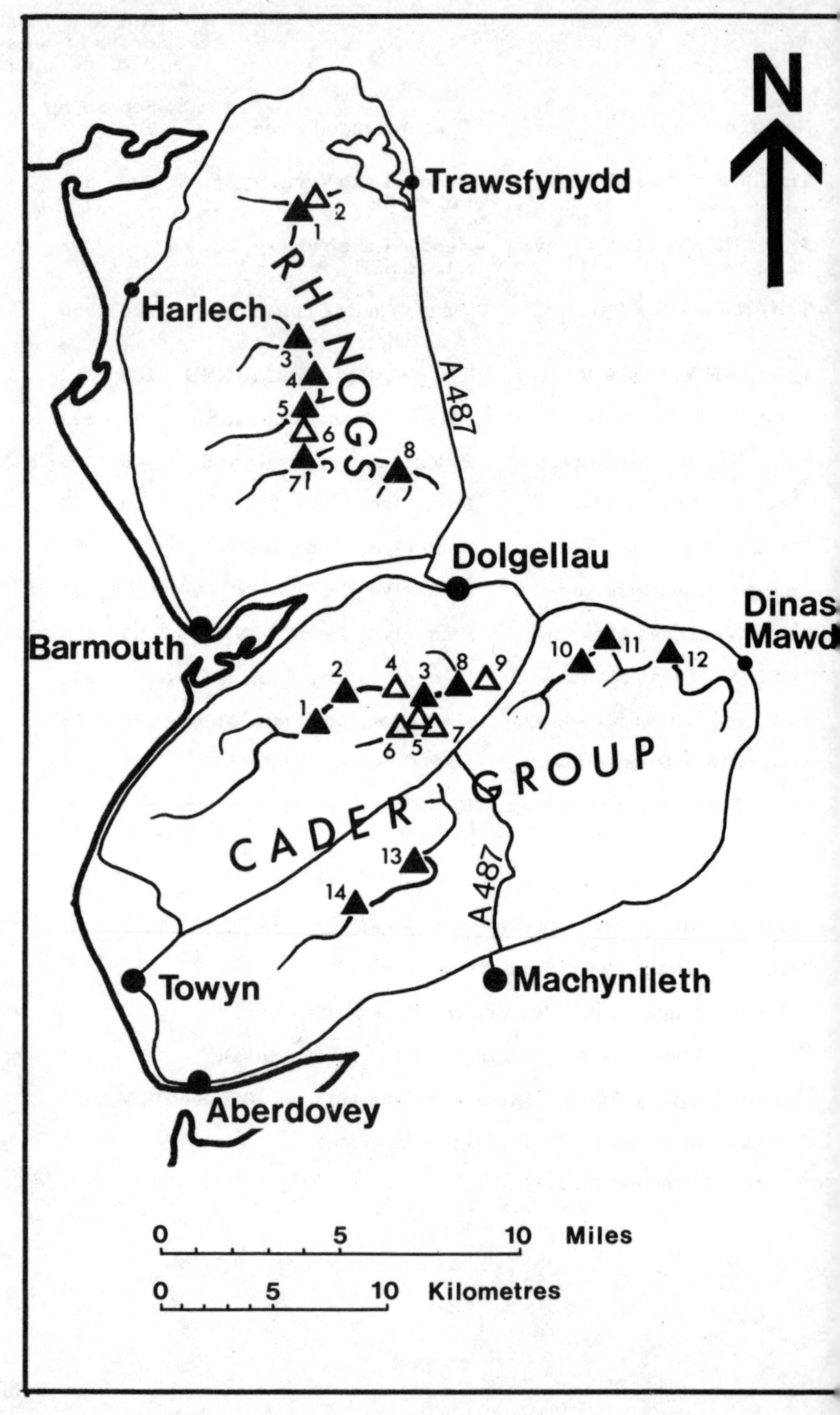

N
Trawsfynydd
RHINOGS
Harlech
A 487
Dolgellau
Dinas Mawd
Barmouth
CADER GROUP
Towyn
Machynlleth
A 487
Aberdovey
0 5 10 Miles
0 5 10 Kilometres

NORTH WALES:

THE RHINOGS
CADER IDRIS GROUP

THE RHINOGS

1 Moel Ysgyfarnogod
2 Foel Penolau
3 Rhinog Fawr
4 Rhinog Fach
5 Y Llethr
6 Crib-y-rhiw
7 Diffwys
8 Y Garn

CADER IDRIS GROUP

1 Craig-y-llyn
2 Tyrau Mawr
3 Cader Idris
4 Cyfrwy
5 Craig Cwm Amarch
6 Mynydd Pencoed
7 Craig Lŵyd
8 Mynydd Moel
9 Mynydd Gwerngraig
10 Waun-oer
11 Cribin Fawr
12 Maesglasau
13 Tarren y Gesail
14 Tarrenhendre

Separate Mountain

Subsidiary Mountain

THE RHINOGS

Name	Height feet metres		Maps 1" 2½" T[1]	Grid Ref.	County
Moel Ysgyfarnogod	2044[2]	623	116 SH63 T	658345	Merionethshire
Foel Penolau[6]	2000+	610+	116 SH63 T	661348	Merionethshire
Rhinog Fawr	2362	720	116 SH62 T	656290	Merionethshire
Rhinog Fach	2333	711	116 SH62 T	664270	Merionethshire
Y Llethr	2475	754	116 SH62 T	661257	Merionethshire
Crib-y-rhiw	2228[6]	679	116 SH62 T	661250	Merionethshire
Diffwys	2462	750	116 SH62 T	661234	Merionethshire
Y Garn	2063	629	116 SH72 T	702230	Merionethshire

Notes

[1] All the summits are in the area shown on the Snowdonia National Park Half-inch Tourist Map.

[2] Half-inch Tourist Map.

[6] Six-inch Map.

| | | No. in order of Altitude | | Date Asc- ended |
Position	Best Ascended From	Sep. Mtn.	Top	
3 mi. W of Trawsfynydd village	Unclassified road, 2¼ mi. to E	222	354	
3 mi. W of Trawsfynydd village	Unclassified road, 2 mi. to E	-	399	
5 mi. ESE of Harlech	Cwm Bychan, 1½ mi. to NNW	113	170	
5¾ mi. SE of Harlech	Cwm Nantcol, 1½ mi. to W	122	185	
7 mi. NNE of Barmouth	Cwm Nantcol, 1½ mi. to NW	89	136	
6½ mi. NNE of Barmouth	Cwm Nantcol, 2 mi. to NW	-	242	
5½ mi. NE of Barmouth	Bontddu, 3 mi. to S	92	139	
3½ mi. NNW of Dolgellau	Caegwernog, 1 mi. to SSE	213	338	

CADER IDRIS GROUP

Name	Height feet	metres	Maps 1" 2½" T[1]	Grid Ref.	County
Craig-y-llyn	2040	622	116 SH61 T	665119	Merionethshire
Tyrau Mawr[2]	2167	661	116 SH61 T	676135	Merionethshire
Cader Idris, Penygadair[3]	2927	892	116 SH71 T	711130	Merionethshire
Cyfrwy (The Saddle)	2646	807	116 SH71 T	703132	Merionethshire
Craig Cwm Amarch[4]	2617[6]	798	116 SH71 T	709122	Merionethshire
Mynydd Pencoed[5]	2513[6]	766	116 SH71 T	704116	Merionethshire
Craig Lŵyd	2251	686	116 SH71 T	714118	Merionethshire
Mynydd Moel	2804	855	116 SH71 T	727136	Merionethshire
Mynydd Gwerngraig[7]	2250	686	116 SH71 T	736136	Merionethshire
Waun-oer	2198[9]	670	116 SH71 T	785147	Merionethshire
Cribin Fawr	2093	638	116 SH71 T	797154	Merionethshire
Maesglasau[8]	2213	675	116 SH81 T	822151	Merionethshire
Tarren y Gesail	2186	666	127 SH70 T	710058	Merionethshire
Tarrenhendre	2076	633	127 SH60 T	683039	Merionethshire

<u>Notes</u>

[1] All the summits are in the area shown on the Snowdonia National Park Half-inch Tourist Map.

[2] Also: Craig-las.

[3] Also: Pen y Gader.

[4] "Mynydd Pencoed" of Rooke Corbett 1929 and E. Moss 1940.

[5] "SW Top" in E. Moss's list.

[6] Six-inch Map.

[7] Also: "Gau Craig" (E. Moss).

[8] Also: Maen Du; and "Maes-glase" (Docharty).

[9] Half-inch Tourist Map.

128

Position	Best Ascended From	No. in order of Altitude		Date Asc-
		Sep. Mtn.	Top	
$5\frac{1}{4}$ mi. SW of Dolgellau	Hafotty-fâch, 1 mi. to NW	223	356	
4 mi. SW of Dolgellau	Hafotty-fâch, 1 mi. to W	184	282	
3 mi. SSW of Dolgellau	Gwernwan Lake Hotel, $1\frac{3}{4}$ mi. to NW	26	31	
$3\frac{1}{4}$ mi. SW of Dolgellau	Gwernan Lake Hotel, $1\frac{3}{4}$ mi. to N	-	82	
$3\frac{3}{4}$ mi. SSW of Dolgellau	Minffordd, $1\frac{1}{2}$ mi. to ESE	-	93	
4 mi. SSW of Dolgellau	Minffordd, $1\frac{3}{4}$ mi. to E	-	123	
$3\frac{3}{4}$ mi. SSW of Dolgellau	Minffordd, $1\frac{1}{4}$ mi. to E	-	224	
$2\frac{1}{2}$ mi. S of Dolgellau	Minffordd, $1\frac{1}{4}$ mi. to SSE	38	51	
$2\frac{1}{2}$ mi. SSE of Dolgellau	Minffordd, $1\frac{1}{4}$ mi. to SSW	-	230	
4 mi. SE of Dolgellau	Cross Foxes (farm), $1\frac{3}{4}$ mi. to NW	170	265	
$4\frac{1}{2}$ mi. ESE of Dolgellau	Cross Foxes (farm), 2 mi. to NNW	206	326	
6 mi. ESE of Dolgellau	Pont Buarth-glas, $\frac{3}{4}$ mi. to NNE	162	250	
4 mi. NW of Machynlleth	Bryneglwys, 1 mi. to WSW	176	272	
$4\frac{1}{4}$ mi. WNW of Machynlleth	Bryneglwys, 1 mi. to NE	210	334	

CENTRAL WALES

Between the Rivers Dovey and Wye lies a vast region of turbulent hills of generally moderate elevation. Owing to its intricate structure, useful boundaries within the region are unusually hard to find and are fortunately hardly necessary, as the eleven two-thousanders in the region rise in three well-separated groups.

The Pumlumon group occupies a high tract of country near the headwaters of the Rivers Severn and Wye. Pen Pumlumon Fawr itself - it was at one time known as "Plynlimmon", a rather poor English attempt to render its Welsh name - is the highest eminence in Central Wales.   The nearest towns and villages are Machynlleth, Llangurig and Devil's Bridge.

The uplands grouped around the Elan valley and called here for convenience the Rhayader Mountains manage to lift three of their number above the 2,000-foot level, and so gain a place in this book. Everything about these mountains is muted and gentle and both the views and the walking distances are long. The nearest town is Rhayader and the nearest village Elan Village. Builth Wells and Llanwrtyd Wells are much farther away.

Much more compact is the Radnor Forest group which occupies a rather pleasant triangle of high land north of the village of New Radnor. The nearest town is Llandrindod Wells.

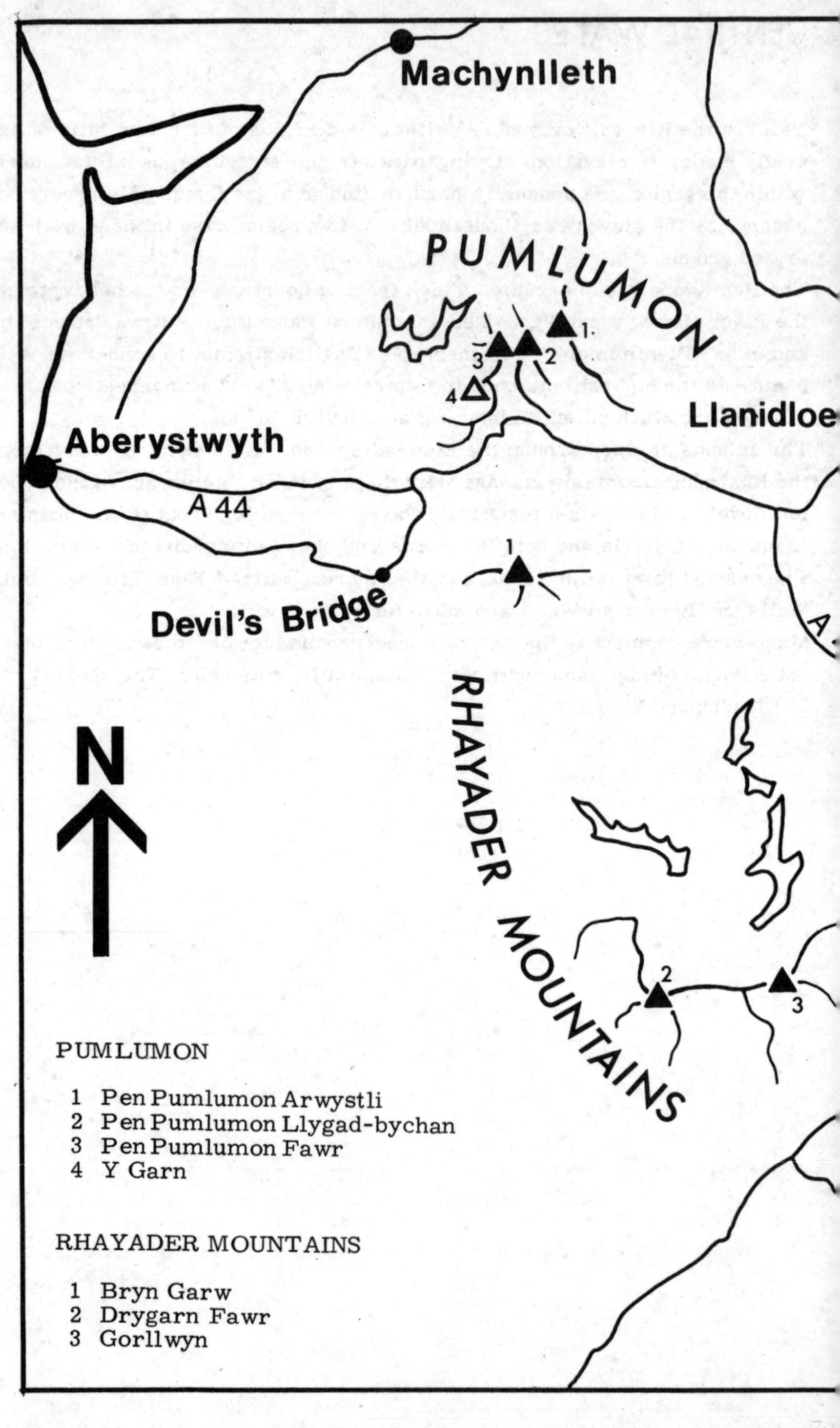

PUMLUMON

1 Pen Pumlumon Arwystli
2 Pen Pumlumon Llygad-bychan
3 Pen Pumlumon Fawr
4 Y Garn

RHAYADER MOUNTAINS

1 Bryn Garw
2 Drygarn Fawr
3 Gorllwyn

CENTRAL WALES:

PUMLUMON
RHAYADER MOUNTAINS
RADNOR FOREST

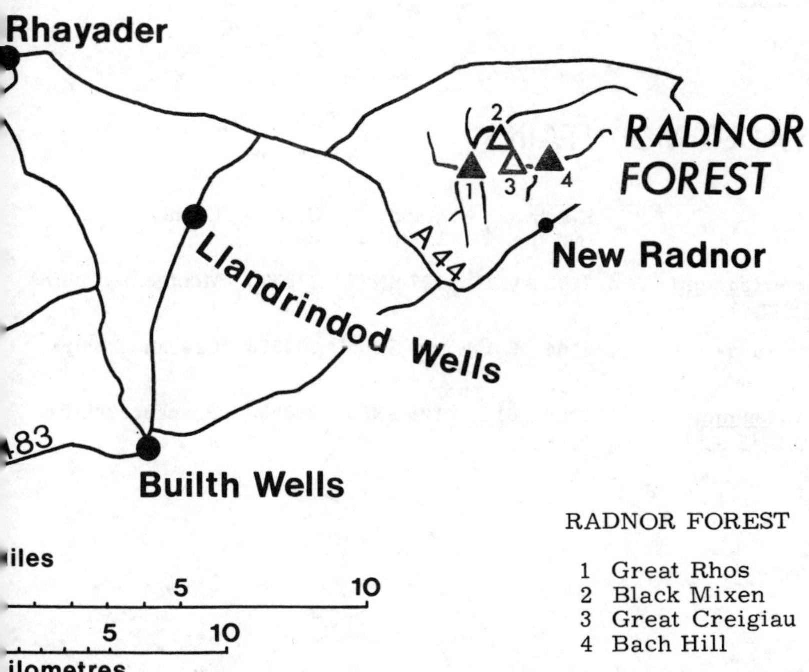

PUMLUMON

Name	Height		Maps		Grid	County
	feet	metres	1" 2½" T		Ref.	
Pen Pumlumon Arwystli[1]	2427	740	127 SN88		815877	Cardiganshire and Montgomeryshire
Pen pumlumon Llygad-bychan[2]	2372[6]	723	127 SN88		802874	Cardiganshire and Montgomeryshire
Pen Pumlumon Fawr[3]	2468	752	127 SN78		789869	Cardiganshire
Y Garn	2245	684	127 SN78		775851	Cardiganshire

<u>Notes</u>

[1] The source (Blaenhafren) of the River Severn (Afon Hafren) is on this mountain, about 2 miles to the NE.

[2] Author's temporary name, from the Llyn Llygad-bychan to the E of the summit (Six-inch Map). The source of the river Wye (Afon Gwy) is on this mountain, a few hundred yards to the SW of the summit.

[3] Cardiganshire County Top.

[6] Six-inch Map.

RHAYADER MOUNTAINS

Name	Height		Maps		Grid	County
	feet	metres	1" 2½" T		Ref.	
Bryn Garw (<u>summit</u> = Pen y Garn[6])	2003	611	127 SN77		798770	Montgomeryshire
Drygarn Fawr	2104	641	140 SN85		862583	Brecknockshire
Gorllwyn (<u>summit</u> = Pen y Gorllywn[6])	2009	612	128 SN95		918590	Brecknockshire

<u>Note</u>

[6] Six-inch map.

Position	Best Ascended From	No. in order of Altitude		Date Asc- ended
		Sep. Mtn.	Top	
9 mi. SSE of Machynlleth	Nant-y-moch Reservoir dam, 3¾ mi. to WSW	99	149	
9 mi. SSE of Machynlleth	Nant-y-moch Reservoir dam, 3 mi. to WSW	111	168	
9 mi. SSE of Machynlleth	Nant-y-moch Reservoir dam, 2 mi. to WSW	91	138	
9¾ mi. S of Machynlleth	Nant-y-moch Reservoir dam, 1½ mi. to WNW	-	233	
3½ mi. E of Devil's Bridge; 12 mi. WNW of Rhayader	Cwmystwyth, 2 mi. to SSW	239	389	
9 mi. SW of Rhayader	Camddwr Bleiddiad, 2½ mi. to SW	201	318	
6½ mi. SW of Rhayader	Llannerch-y-cawr, 2 mi. to NW	237	385	

RADNOR FOREST

Name	Height		Maps			Grid	County
	feet	metres	1"	2½" T		Ref.	
Great Rhos[1]	2166	660	128	SO16		182638	Radnorshire
Black Mixen	2135	651	128	SO16		196643	Radnorshire
Great Creigiau	2102[2]	641	128	SO16		197635	Radnorshire
Bach Hill	2002	610	128	SO26		214636	Radnorshire

Notes

[1] Radnorshire County Top.

[2] 1:25000 (2½") map.

Position	Best Ascended From	No. in order of Altitude		Date Ascended
		Sep. Mtn.	Top	
7½ mi. ENE of Llandrindod Wells	New Radnor, 2½ mi. to SE	185	284	
8½ mi. ENE of Llandrindod Wells	New Radnor, 2¼ mi. to SSE	-	304	
8½ mi. ENE of Llandrindod Wells	New Radnor, 1¾ mi. to SSE	-	319	
9½ mi. E of Llandrindod Wells	New Radnor, 1½ mi. to S	241	392	

SOUTH WALES

The mountains in this southern region of Wales form several quite distinct massifs, two of which contain all the region's thirty-one two-thousander peaks. The Brecon Beacons consist essentially of a twenty-five-mile long serrated scarp facing north and overlooking the Brecon basin. An intricate ridge links the many fine mountains along its lip.

East of the Brecon basin an extraordinary group of mountains takes in plan the form of a gigantic hand whose long, knuckled fingers all point to the south-east. These are the Black Mountains. This remarkable series of mountain ridges changes little in altitude in the course of many miles, and thus gives rise to unique problems when, as for the purposes of this book, it is required to distinguish between "separate mountains" and "subsidiary tops".

The town of Brecon is by far the best centre for both of these groups of mountains; other towns and villages nearby include Llandovery, Abergavenny, Talgarth and Hay-on-Wye.

Pen-y-Fan, Brecon Beacons

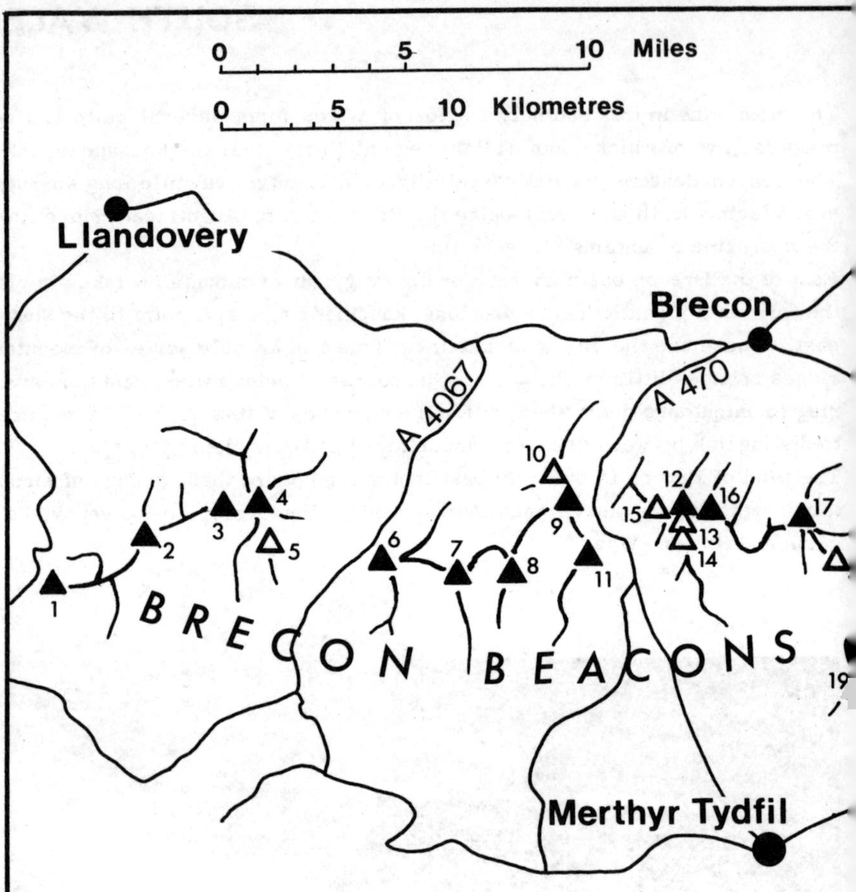

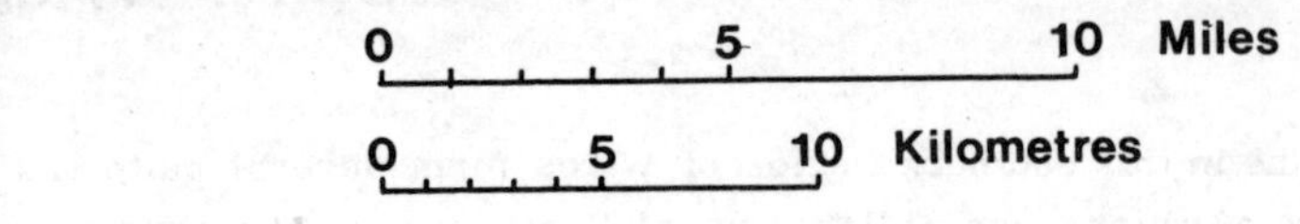

1 Garreg-lwyd
2 Gareg Lâs
3 Bannau Sir Gaer
4 Bannau Brycheiniog
5 Fan Hir
6 Fan Gihirych
7 Fan Nedd
8 Fan Llia
9 Rhôs Dringarth

10 Fan Frynych
11 Fan Fawr
12 Pen y Fan
13 Corn Dû
14 Duwynt
15 Y Gyrn
16 Cribin
17 Waen-rydd
18 Allt Lwyd
19 Cefn yr Ystrad

SOUTH WALES:

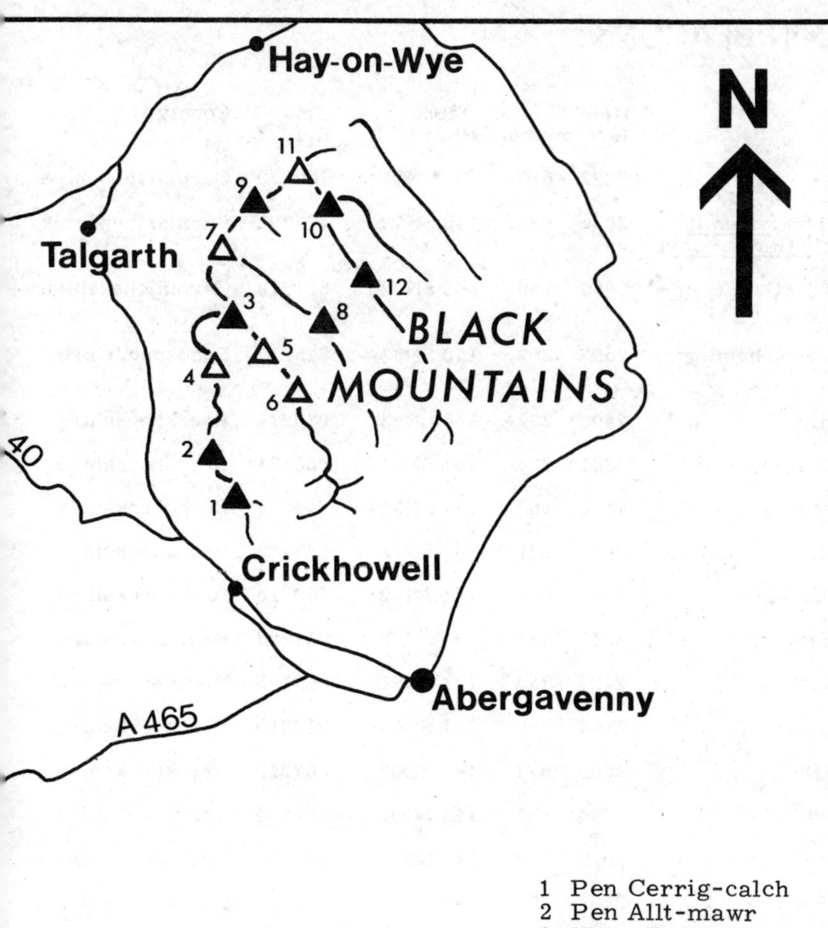

BRECON BEACONS
BLACK MOUNTAINS

BRECON BEACONS

Name	Height feet	metres	Maps 1"	2½" T	Grid Ref.	County
Garreg-lwyd[1]	2022	616	153	SN71	740179	Carmarthenshire
Gareg Lâs (<u>summit = Carnau'r Gareg = lâs</u>)	2076	633	140	SN72	777202	Carmarthenshire
Bannau Sir Gaer (<u>summit = Picws Du[6]</u>)	2460	750	140	SN82	811218	Carmarthenshire
Bannau Brycheiniog[2]	2632	802	140	SN82	825217	Brecknockshire
Fan Hir	2400+	732+	140	SN82	830210	Brecknockshire
Fan Gihirych	2381	726	141	SN81	880191	Brecknockshire
Fan Nedd	2176	663	141	SN91	913184	Brecknockshire
Fan Llia	2071	631	141	SN91	937185	Brecknockshire
Rhôs Dringarth[3]	2060	628	141	SN92	960216	Brecknockshire
Fan Frynych	2047	624	141	SN92	957227	Brecknockshire
Fan Fawr	2409	734	141	SN91	969193	Brecknockshire
Pen y Fan[4]	2906	886	141	SO02	012215	Brecknockshire
Corn Dû[5]	2863	873	141	SO02	007213	Brecknockshire
Duwynt[7]	2704	824	141	SO02	005206	Brecknockshire
Y Gyrn	2010	613	141	SN92	988217	Brecknockshire
Cribin[8]	2608	795	141	SO02	023213	Brecknockshire
Waen-rydd[9]	2504	763	141	SO02	061208	Brecknockshire
Allt Lwyd	2143[6]	653	141	SO01	079189	Brecknockshire
Cefn yr Ystrad[10]	2000+	610+	141	SO01	087136	Brecknockshire

Position	Best Ascended From	No. in order of Altitude		Date Ascended
		Sep. Mtn.	Top	
10 mi. S of Llandovery	A. 4069 road, $\frac{3}{4}$ mi. to W	230	375	
9 mi. S of Llandovery	Penmaen, 2 mi. to NW	209	333	
8 mi. SSE of Llandovery	Unclassified road, $1\frac{1}{2}$ mi. to NW	94	141	
$8\frac{1}{2}$ mi. SSE of Llandovery	Unclassified road, $2\frac{1}{4}$ mi. to NW	59	86	
9 mi. SSE of Llandovery	Gwyn Arms, 3 mi. to SSE	-	160	
12 mi. SW of Brecon	A. 4067 road, $\frac{3}{4}$ mi. to NW	109	166	
$10\frac{1}{2}$ mi. SW of Brecon	Unclassified road, $\frac{3}{4}$ mi. to E	179	275	
9 mi. SW of Brecon	Unclassified road, 1 mi. to W	211	336	
7 mi. SW of Brecon	A. 470 road, $\frac{3}{4}$ mi. to E	215	341	
$6\frac{1}{2}$ mi. SW of Brecon	A. 470 road, 1 mi. to E	-	352	
$7\frac{1}{2}$ mi. SW of Brecon	A. 470 road, $\frac{3}{4}$ mi. to NE	103	155	
5 mi. SSW of Brecon	A. 470 road, $1\frac{3}{4}$ mi. to SW	28	34	
5 mi. SSW of Brecon	A. 470 road, $1\frac{1}{2}$ mi. to SW	-	39	
$5\frac{1}{2}$ mi. SSW of Brecon	A. 470 road, $1\frac{1}{4}$ mi. to SW	-	72	
$5\frac{1}{2}$ mi. SW of Brecon	A. 470 road, 1 mi. to SW	-	384	
$4\frac{3}{4}$ mi. SSW of Brecon	Bailea, 2 mi. to NNE	65	95	
5 mi. SSE of Brecon	Unclassified road, 2 mi. to S	82	124	
$6\frac{1}{4}$ mi. SSE of Brecon	Unclassified road, $\frac{3}{4}$ mi. to S	-	300	
$9\frac{1}{2}$ mi. SSE of Brecon	Pyrgad, $1\frac{1}{2}$ mi. to NE	245	397	

<u>Notes</u>

[1] Also "Moel Gornach" (E. Moss).

[2] Also: Carmarthen Van. The summit is not in Carmarthenshire, though the boundary and County Top is not far away.

[3] Six-inch map.   Also: Craig Cerrig-gleisiad (Docharty and E. Moss).

[4] Brecon Beacons (E. Moss).   The Brecon Beacons strictly include also Corn Du, Duwynt, Y Gyrn, Cribin and possibly also Waen-rydd. Pen y Fan is Brecknockshire County Top.

[5] "Cairn Du" of Rooke Corbett's list, 1911.

[6] Six-inch map.

[7] Docharty, E. Moss and Rooke Corbett.

[8] Bryn Teg (Docharty, Rooke Corbett and E. Moss).   However, Bryn Teg is merely the long NE grassy slope; Cribin is the "rake" at the top.

[9] Twin summits, the SE one, nearly a mile away and at much the same altitude, being connected by a shallow col.

[10] Also: Mynydd Llangynidr.

BLACK MOUNTAINS

Name	Height feet	metres	Maps 1"	2½" T	Grid Ref.	County
Pen Cerrig-calch	2302	702	141	SO22	217223	Brecknockshire
Pen Allt-mawr	2360	719	141	SO22	206243	Brecknockshire
Waun Fach	2660	811	141	SO22	215299	Brecknockshire
Mynydd Llysiau	2173	662	141	SO22	207278	Brecknockshire
Pen y Gader-Fawr	2624	800	141	SO22	229287	Brecknockshire
Pen-twŷn-mawr[1]	2154	657	141	SO22	242266	Brecknockshire
Rhos Dirion[2]	2338	713	141	SO23	211334	Brecknockshire
Chwarel y Fan[3]	2228	679	141	SO22	257294	Brecknockshire and Monmouthshire
The Tumpa[4]	2263	690	141	SO23	225349	Brecknockshire
Black Mountain[5]	2306	703	141	SO23	255350	Brecknockshire and Herefordshire
Pen y Beacon[7]	2219	676	141	SO23	244366	Brecknockshire
Pen y Garn Fawr[8]	2003	611	142	SO23	281307	Herefordshire and Monmouthshire

<u>Notes</u>

[1] Decided from 1:25000 (2½") map contours.

[2] Decided from 1:25000 (2½") map contours.   "Pen Rhos Dirion" (E. Moss).

[3] Monmouthshire County Top. "Fwddog Ridge, (Frontier)" in Elmslie's list.

[4] "Lord Hereford's Knob" on Bartholomew's Half-inch map.

[5] Herefordshire County Top.

[7] Also: Hay Bluff.

[8] Temporary name.   Docharty's suggested name for this peak.

Position	Best Ascended From	No. in order of Altitude		Date Ascended
		Sep. Mtn.	Top	
2½ mi. N of Crickhowell	Crickhowell, 2½ mi. to S	135	202	
3½ mi. N of Crickhowell	Cwmdu, 1¾ mi. to W	114	173	
4¼ mi. SE of Talgarth	Unclassified road, 2 mi. to NW	54	80	
5 mi. SE of Talgarth	A. 479 road, 1¼ mi. to W	-	279	
5½ mi. SE of Talgarth	Unclassified road, 2 mi. to S	-	90	
7 mi. SE of Talgarth	Unclassified road, ¾ mi. to E	-	292	
3½ mi. E of Talgarth	Unclassified road, ¾ mi. to NW	-	182	
7 mi. ESE of Talgarth	Unclassified road, 1 mi. to NE	155	241	
4½ mi. S of Hay-on-Wye	Gospel Pass, ½ mi. to E	146	220	
5 mi. SSE of Hay-on-Wye	Unclassified road, 1 mi. to W	131	197	
3¾ mi. SSE of Hay-on-Wye	Unclassified road, ½ mi. to W	-	244	
10½ mi. N of Abergavenny	Unclassified road, ½ mi. to NE	240	391	

TABLE 2   MOUNTAINS IN ORDER ALTITUDE

Sep. Mtn.	Top	Name	Group	Height feet	Height metres
1	1	Y Wyddfa (Snowdon)	Snowdon	3560	1085
2	2	Crib-y-ddysgl	Snowdon	3496	1066
3	3	Carnedd Llywelyn	Carneddau	3485	1062
4	4	Carnedd Dafydd	Carneddau	3424	1044
5	5	Glyder Fawr	Glyders	3279	999
6	6	Glyder Fâch	Glyders	3262	994
7	7	Pen-yr-oleu-wen	Carneddau	3211	979
8	8	Scafell Pike	Scafell	3210	978
9	9	Foel-grach	Carneddau	3196	974
10	10	Scafell	Scafell	3162	964
11	11	Yr Elen	Carneddau	3152	961
12	12	Helvellyn	Helvellyn	3116	949
13	13	Y Garn	Glyders	3104	946
14	14	Foel-fras	Carneddau	3092	942
-	15	Broad Crag, Scafell Pike	Scafell	3054	931
15	16	Skiddaw	Skiddaw	3054	931
-	17	Lower Man, Helvellyn	Helvellyn	3033	924
16	18	Elidir Fawr	Glyders	3030	924
17	19	Crib-goch	Snowdon	3026	922
-	20	Ill Crag, Scafell Pike	Scafell	3025+	922+
18	21	Tryfan	Glyders	3010	917
19	22	Great End	Scafell	2984	910
-	23	Garnedd-uchaf, - Foel-grach	Carneddau	c. 2980	c. 908
20	24	Aran Fawddwy	Arans	2974	906
21	25	Bowfell	Scafell	2960	902
-	26	Blunt Top, Scafell Pike	Scafell	2950+	899+
22	27	Great Gable	Great Gable	2949	899
23	28	Y Lliwedd	Snowdon	2947	898
24	29	Cross Fell	Cross Fell	2930	893
25	30	Pillar Fell	Great Gable	2928	892
26	31	Cader Idris	Cader Idris	2927	892
-	32	Nethermost Pike, - Helvellyn	Helvellyn	2920	890
27	33	Catstye Cam	Helvellyn	2917	889
28	34	Pen y Fan	Brecon Beacons	2906	886

29	35	Esk Pike	Scafell	2903	885
30	36	Aran Benllyn	Arans	2901	884
-	37	High Crag, Helvellyn	Helvellyn	2896	883
31	38	Raise	Helvellyn	2889	881
-	39	Corn Dû, Pen y Fan	Brecon Beacons	2863	873
32	40	Fairfield	Helvellyn	2863	873
33	41	Moel Siabod	Moel Siabod	2861	872
34	42	Blencathra	Skiddaw	2847	868
-	43	Erw y Ddafad-ddu, - Aran Benllyn	Arans	2838	865
-	44	Little Man, Skiddaw	Skiddaw	2837	865
-	45	Striding Edge, Helvellyn	Helvellyn	2832	863
-	46	White Side, Raise	Helvellyn	2832	863
-	47	Bowfell North, Bowfell	Scafell	2825	861
35	48	Crinkle Crags	Scafell	2816	858
36	49	Dollywaggon Pike	Helvellyn	2810	856
37	50	Gread Dodd	Helvellyn	2807	856
38	51	Mynydd Moel	Cader Idris	2804	855
39	52	Arennig Fawr	Arennigs	2801	854
40	53	Grasmoor	Buttermere	2791	851
41	54	Great Dun Fell	Cross Fell	2780	847
-	55	Pen-aran, Aran Benllyn	Arans	2775	846
42	56	Stybarrow Dod	Helvellyn	c. 2770	c. 844
-	57	Little Dun Fell, - Great Dun Fell	Cross Fell	2761	842
43	58	Little Scoat Fell	Great Gable	2760	841
44	59	St. Sunday Crag	Helvellyn	2756	840
45	60	Crag Hill	Buttermere	2753	839
-	61	Great Scoat Fell, - Little Scoat Fell	Great Gable	2750+	838+
-	62	Llwytmor, Foel-fras	Carneddau	2750+	838+
-	63	Middle Scoat Fell, - Little Scoat Fell	Great Gable	2750+	838+
-	64	Flesk, Crinkle Crags	Scafell	2733	833
46	65	Pen yr Helgi-du	Carneddau	2733	833
-	66	Pen y Diocyn, - Arennig Fawr	Arennigs	2731	832
47	67	Foel-goch	Glyders	2727	831
48	68	High Street	High Street	2719	829
49	69	Moel Sych	Berwyns	2713	827
-	70	Cadair Berwyn, Moel Sych	Berwyns	2712	827
50	71	Red Pike (Wasdale)	Great Gable	2707	825
-	72	Duwynt, Pen y Fan	Brecon Beacons	2704	824

-	73	Moel Llechwedd, - Arennig Fawr	Arennigs	2700+	823+
51	74	Hart Crag	Helvellyn	2698	822
52	75	Carnedd y Filiast	Glyders	2695	821
-	76	Steeple, Little Scoat Fell	Great Gable	2687	819
53	77	The Cheviot	Cheviots	2674	815
-	78	Shelter Crags, - Crinkle Crags	Scafell	2667	813
-	79	Mynydd Perfedd, - Carnedd y Filiast	Glyders	2665	812
54	80	Waun Fach	Black Mountains	2660	811
55	81	Lingmell	Scafell	2649	807
-	82	Cyfrwy, Cader Idris	Cader Idris	2646	807
56	83	High Stile	Great Gable	2644	806
57	84	Moel Nant yr Ogof	Glyders	2642	805
58	85	High Raise	High Street	2634	803
59	86	Bannau Brycheiniog	Brecon Beacons	2632	802
60	87	The Old Man of Coniston	Coniston	2631	802
61	88	Kirk Fell West	Great Gable	2630	802
62	89	Swirl How	Coniston	2630	802
-	90	Pen y Gader-Fawr, - Waun Fach	Black Mountains	2624	800
63	91	Pen Llithrig y Wrâch	Carneddau	2622	799
64	92	Haycock	Great Gable	2618	798
-	93	Craig Cwm Amarch, - Cader Idris	Cader Idris	2617	798
-	94	Brim Fell, The Old Man of Coniston	Coniston	2611	796
65	95	Cribin	Brecon Beacons	2608	795
66	96	Knock Fell	Cross Fell	2604	794
-	97	Dove Crag, Hart Crag	Helvellyn	2603	793
-	98	Green Gable, Great Gable	Great Gable	2603	793
-	99	Green Side, Stybarrow Dod	Helvellyn	2600	792
67	100	Grisedale Pike	Buttermere	2593	790
68	101	Mickle Fell	Cross Fell	2591	790
-	102	Rampsgill Head, - High Raise	High Street	2581	787
-	103	Kirk Fell East, - Kirk Fell West	Great Gable	2579	786
-	104	Great Carrs, Swirl How	Coniston	2575	785
69	105	Allen Crags	Scafell	2572	784
70	106	Cadair Bronwen	Berwyns	2572	784
-	107	Thornthwaite Crag, - High Street	High Street	2569	783
71	108	Moel Hebog	Moel Hebog	2568	783

72	109	Glaramara	Scafell	2560	780
73	110	Glasgwm	Arans	2557	779
74	111	Dow Crag	Coniston	2555	779
-	112	Looking Stead, - Glaramara	Scafell	2500+	777+
75	113	Kilnshaw Chimney	Helvellyn	2547	776
76	114	Harter Fell	High Street	2539	774
77	115	Grey Friar	Coniston	2536	773
-	116	Wanlope, Crag Hill	Buttermere	2533	772
-	117	Sail, Crag Hill	Buttermere	c. 2530	c. 771
78	118	Drum	Carneddau	2529	771
79	119	Moelwyn Mawr	Moel Siabod	2527	770
80	120	Hopegill Head	Buttermere	2525	770
81	121	Meldon Hill	Cross Fell	2518	767
-	122	Great Rigg, Fairfield	Helvellyn	2513	766
-	123	Mynydd Pencoed, - Cader Idris	Cader Idris	2513	766
82	124	Waen-rydd	Brecon Beacons	2504	763
83	125	Stony Cove Pike	High Street	2502	763
84	126	Wetherlam	Coniston	2502	763
-	127	Pillar Rock, Pillar Fell	Great Gable	2500+	762+
85	128	High Raise	Scafell	2500	762
-	129	Gallt yr Ogof, - Moel Nant yr Ogof	Glyders	2499	762
-	130	Slight Side, Scafell	Scafell	2499	762
-	131	Mardale Ill Bell, - High Street	High Street	2496	761
86	132	Drosgl	Carneddau	2484	757
-	133	Hart Side, Stybarrow Dod	Helvellyn	2481	756
87	134	Red Pike (Ennerdale)	Great Gable	2479	756
88	135	Ill Bell, Kentmere	High Street	2476	755
89	136	Y Llethr	Rhinogs	2475	754
90	137	Dale Head	Buttermere	2473	754
91	138	Pen Pumlumon Fawr	Pumlumon	2468	752
92	139	Diffwys	Rhinogs	2462	750
93	140	Moel Llyfnant	Arennigs	2461	750
94	141	Bannau Sir Gaer	Brecon Beacons	2460	750
95	142	Burnhope Seat	Burnhope Seat	2452	747
96	143	Yr Aran	Snowdon	2451	747
97	144	Little Fell	Cross Fell	2446	746
-	145	Black Sails, Wetherlam	Coniston	2443	745
98	146	High Crag	Great Gable	2443	745
-	147	Hangingstone Hill, - The Cheviot	Cheviots	2433	742

-	148	Tomle, Moel Sych	Berwyns	2431	741
99	149	Pen Pumlumon Arwystli	Pumlumon	2427	740
-	150	The Knott, High Raise	High Street	2423	739
-	151	Carl Side, Skiddaw	Skiddaw	c. 2420	c. 738
100	152	Whernside	Ingleborough	2419	737
101	153	Robinson	Buttermere	2417	737
102	154	Seat Sandal	Helvellyn	2415	736
103	155	Fan Fawr	Brecon Beacons	2409	734
104	156	Rhobell Fawr	Arennigs	2409	734
105	157	Craig Cwm Silyn	Moel Hebog	2408	734
-	158	Long Side, Skiddaw	Skiddaw	2405	733
-	159	Harrison Stickle, - High Raise	Scafell	2403	732
-	160	Fan Hir, - Bannau Brycheiniog	Brecon Beacons	2400+	732+
-	161	Kentmere Pike, - Harter Fell	High Street	2397	731
106	162	Hindscarth	Buttermere	2385	727
-	163	Auchope Cairn, - The Cheviot	Cheviots	2382	726
107	164	Moel Eilio	Snowdon	2382	726
108	165	Clough Head	Helvellyn	2381	726
109	166	Fan Gihirych	Brecon Beacons	2381	726
110	167	Ingleborough Hill	Ingleborough	2373	723
111	168	Pen Pumlumon Llygad-bychan	Pumlumon	2372	723
112	169	Ullscarf	Scafell	2370	722
113	170	Rhinog Fawr	Rhinogs	2362	720
-	171	Thunacar Knott, - High Raise	Scafell	2362	720
-	172	Lincombe Tarns, - Glaramara	Scafell	2360	719
114	173	Pen Allt-mawr	Black Mountains	2360	719
-	174	Froswick, Ill Bell, - Kentmere	High Street	2359	719
115	175	Llechog	Snowdon	2359	719
-	176	Birkhouse Moor, - Helvellyn	Helvellyn	2353	717
116	177	Brandreth	Great Gable	2344	714
117	178	Lonscale Fell	Skiddaw	2344	714
118	179	Hedgehope Hill	Cheviots	2343	714
-	180	Redgleam, Burnhope Seat	Burnhope Seat	2342	714
119	181	Great Shunner Fell	Great Shunner	2340	713
-	182	Rhos Dirion, Waun Fach	Black Mountains	2338	713
120	183	Moelwyn Bach	Moel Siabod	2334	711

121	184	Branstree	High Street	**2333**	711
122	185	Rhinog Fach	Rhinogs	2333	711
123	186	Melmerby Fell	Cross Fell	2331	710
124	187	Knott	Skiddaw	2329	710
125	188	Trum y Ddysgl	Moel Hebog	2329	710
126	189	High Seat	Great Shunner	2328	710
-	190	Dead Stones, - Burnhope Seat	Burnhope Seat	2326	709
127	191	Wild Boar Fell	Great Shunner	2324	708
-	192	Pike o' Stickle, - High Raise	Scafell	2323	708
128	193	High Field	Burnhope Seat	2322	708
129	194	Whiteside	Buttermere	2317	706
130	195	Great Whernside	Ingleborough	2310	704
-	196	Yoke, Ill Bell, Kentmere	High Street	2309	704
131	197	Black Mountain	Black Mountains	2306	703
132	198	Bowscale Fell	Skiddaw	2306	703
133	199	Pike o' Blisco	Scafell	2304	702
134	200	Buckden Pike	Ingleborough	2302	702
-	201	Garnedd-goch, - Craig Cwm Silyn	Moel Hebog	2302	702
135	202	Pen Cerrig-calch	Black Mountains	2302	702
-	203	Ladyside Pike, - Hopegill Head	Buttermere	2300+	701
136	204	Chapelfell Top	Burnhope Seat	2297	700
137	205	Backstone Edge	Cross Fell	2292	699
138	206	Mynydd Mawr	Moel Hebog	2290	698
-	207	Caw Fell, Haycock	Great Gable	2288	697
139	208	Allt Fawr	Moel Siabod	2287	697
-	209	Grey Knotts, Brandreth	Great Gable	2287	697
-	210	Mynydd Drws-y-coed, - Trum y Ddysgl	Moel Hebog	2286	697
-	211	Fendrith Hill, - Chapelfell Top	Burnhope Seat	2284	696
140	212	Rest Dodd	High Street	2278	694
-	213	Carnedd y Ddelw, Drum	Carneddau	2275+	693+
141	214	Penyghent Hill	Ingleborough	2273	693
-	215	Loft Crag, High Raise	Scafell	c. 2270	c. 692
142	216	Seatallan	Great Gable	2270	692
143	217	Cnicht	Moel Siabod	2265	690
144	218	Foel Wen	Berwyns	2265	690
145	219	Great Calva	Skiddaw	2265	690
146	220	The Tumpa	Black Mountains	2263	690
147	221	Arennig Fach	Arennigs	2259	689

-	222	Cold Pike, Crinkle Crags	Scafell	2259	689
-	223	Hugh Seat, High Seat	Great Shunner	2257	688
-	224	Craig Lŵyd, Cader Idris	Cader Idris	2251	686
-	225	Archy Styrigg, High Seat	Great Shunner	2250+	686+
148	226	Foel Hafod-fynydd	Arans	2250+	686+
-	227	Long Crag, Mickle Fell	Cross Fell	2250+	686+
-	228	Pen-y-bryn, - Cadair Bronwen	Berwyns	2250+	686+
149	229	Great Coum	Ingleborough	2250+	686
-	230	Mynydd Gwerngraig, - Mynydd Moel	Cader Idris	2250	686
150	231	Round Hill	Cross Fell	2249	685
-	232	Gwaen y Llŵyni, - Aran Fawddwy	Arans	2248	685
-	233	Y Garn, - Pen Pumlumon Fawr	Pumlumon	2245	684
151	234	Moel Poethion	Berwyns	2239	682
152	235	Swarth Fell	Great Shunner	2235	681
153	236	Sheffield Pike	Helvellyn	2232	680
154	237	Plover Hill	Ingleborough	2231	680
-	238	Bannerdale Crags, - Bowscale Fell	Skiddaw	c. 2230	c. 680
-	239	Mynydd Tarw, Foel Wen	Berwyns	2230	680
-	240	Ullock Pike, Skiddaw	Skiddaw	2230	680
155	241	Chwarel y Fan	Black Mountains	2228	679
-	242	Crib-y-rhiw, - Y Llethr	Rhinogs	2228	679
156	243	Godor	Berwyns	2226	678
-	244	Pen y Beacon, - Black Mountain	Black Mountains	2219	676
157	245	The Calf	Great Shunner	2219	676
158	246	James's Hill	Burnhope Seat	2216	675
159	247	Knoutberry Haw	Great Shunner	2216	675
160	248	Creigiau Gleision	Carneddau	2213	675
161	249	Lovely Seat	Great Shunner	2213	675
162	250	Maesglasau	Cader Idris	2213	675
163	251	Wether Hill	High Street	c. 2210	c. 674
-	252	Nowtli Hill, Branstree	High Street	2209	673
164	253	Killhope Law	Burnhope Seat	2207	673
165	254	Moel y Cynghorion	Snowdon	2207	673
166	255	Murton Fell	Cross Fell	2207	673
167	256	Scar Crags	Buttermere	2205	672
168	257	Great Knoutberry Hill	Ingleborough	2203	671
169	258	Rogan's Seat	Great Shunner	2203	671

-	259	Loadpot Hill, - Wether Hill	High Street	2202	671
-	260	Bram Rigg Top, - The Calf	Great Shunner	2200+	671+
-	261	Calders, The Calf	Great Shunner	2200+	671+
-	262	Sale How, Skiddaw	Skiddaw	2200+	671+
-	263	Tarn Crags Top, - Bowscale Fell	Skiddaw	2200+	671+
-	264	Tarn Rigg Hill, - Knoutberry Haw	Great Shunner	2200+	671+
170	265	Waun-oer	Cader Idris	2198	670
171	266	Gylchedd	Arennigs	2195	669
172	267	Ysgafell Wen	Moel Siabod	2192	668
173	268	Fountains Fell	Ingleborough	2191	668
174	269	Dodd Fell Hill	Ingleborough	2189	667
-	270	Water Crag, Rogan's Seat	Great Shunner	2188	667
175	271	Sails	Great Shunner	2186	666
176	272	Tarren y Gesail	Cader Idris	2186	666
177	273	Cyrniau Nôd	Berwyns	2185	666
178	274	Black Fell	Black Fell	2179	664
179	275	Fan Nedd	Brecon Beacons	2176	663
180	276	Tarn Crag	High Street	2176	663
181	277	White Mossy Hill	Great Shunner	2175+	663+
182	278	Carrock Fell	Skiddaw	2174	663
-	279	Mynydd Llysiau, - Waun Fach	Black Mountains	2173	662
-	280	Nine Standards Rigg, - White Mossy Hill	Great Shunner	2171	662
183	281	Manod Mawr South	Moel Siabod	2167	661
184	282	Tyrau Mawr	Cader Idris	2167	661
-	283	Calfhow Pike, Great Dodd	Helvellyn	2166	660
185	284	Great Rhos	Radnor Forest	2166	660
-	285	Y Groes Fagl, - Cyrniau Nôd	Berwyns	2162	659
-	286	Long Man Hill, Cross Fell	Cross Fell	2160	658
186	287	High Pike	Skiddaw	2159	658
-	288	Whiteless Pike, Crag Hill	Buttermere	2159	658
-	289	Manod Mawr North, - Manod Mawr South	Moel Siabod	2158	658
187	290	Place Fell	High Street	2155	657
188	291	Y Dduallt	Arennigs	2155	657
-	292	Pen-twyn-mawr, - Waun Fach	Black Mountains	2154	657
189	293	Grey Nag	Black Fell	2153	656
-	294	Moel Druman, Allt Fawr	Moel Siabod	2152	656

-	295	Outberry Plain, - James's Hill	Burnhope Seat	2150+	655+
190	296	Pen y Boncyn trefeilw	Berwyns	2150+	655+
191	297	Post Gwyn	Berwyns	2150+	655+
-	298	Pen y Bryn-fforchog, - Glasgwm	Arans	2149	655
192	299	Mynydd Tal-y-mignedd	Moel Hebog	2148	655
-	300	Allt Lwyd, - Waen-rydd	Brecon Beacons	2143	653
193	301	Harter Fell	Coniston	2143	653
194	302	High Spy	Buttermere	2143	653
-	303	Selside Pike, Branstree	High Street	2142	653
-	304	Black Mixen, Great Rhos	Radnor Forest	2135	651
-	305	Rossett Pike, Bowfell	Scafell	2135	651
-	306	Three Pikes, High Field	Burnhope Seat	2133	650
195	307	Comb Fell	Cheviots	2132	650
-	308	Great Sca Fell, Knott	Skiddaw	2131	650
196	309	Trum y Sarn	Berwyns	2127	648
197	310	Fleetwith Pike	Great Gable	2126	648
-	311	Swarth Fell Pike, - Swarth Fell	Great Shunner	2125	648
198	312	Moel-yr-hydd	Moel Siabod	2124	647
-	313	Base Brown, Great Gable	Great Gable	2120	646
-	314	Black Hill, James's Hill	Burnhope Seat	2115	645
199	315	Viewing Hill	Cross Fell	2111	643
-	316	Carnedd Llechwedd, - Gylchedd	Arennigs	2109	643
200	317	Yockenthwaite Moor	Ingleborough	2109	643
201	318	Drygarn Fawr	Rhayader - Mountains	2104	641
-	319	Great Creigiau, - Great Rhos	Radnor Forest	2102	641
202	320	Foel Rhudd	Arans	2100+	640+
203	321	Iron Crag	Great Gable	2100+	640+
-	322	Simon Fell, - Ingleborough Hill	Ingleborough	2100+	640+
-	323	Stac Rhôs, - Pen y Boncyn trefeilw	Berwyns	2100+	640+
204	324	Yarlside	Great Shunner	2097	639
205	325	Moel Lefn	Moel Hebog	2094	638
206	326	Cribin Fawr	Cader Idris	2093	638
-	327	Grey Crag, Tarn Crag	High Street	2093	638
-	328	Little Hart Crag, - Hart Crag	Helvellyn	2091	637
207	329	Kinder Scout	Peak District	2088	636

-	330	Starling Dodd, - Red Pike (Ennerdale)	Great Gable	2085	636
-	331	Y Garn, Trum, y Ddysgl	Moel Hebog	2080	634
208	332	Fiend's Fell	Cross Fell	2079	634
209	333	Gareg Lâs	Brecon Beacons	2076	633
210	334	Tarrenhendre	Cader Idris	2076	633
-	335	Stangend Rigg, - Killhope Law	Burnhope Seat	2075	632
211	336	Fan Llia	Brecon Beacons	2071	631
212	337	Moel Fferna	Berwyns	2071	631
213	338	Y Garn	Rhinogs	2063	629
-	339	Rough Crag, High Street	High Street	2062	628
214	340	Bleaklow	Peak District	2060	628
215	341	Rhôs Dringarth	Brecon Beacons	2060	628
216	342	Gragareth	Ingleborough	2058	627
-	343	Looking Stead, - Pillar Fell	Great Gable	2058	627
217	344	Yewbarrow	Great Gable	2058	627
218	345	Foel y Geifr	Arans	2055	626
-	346	Green Hill, Great Coum	Ingleborough	2054	626
219	347	Fell Head	Great Shunner	2050+	625+
-	348	Foel-gron, Moel Eilio	Snowdon	2050+	625+
-	349	Tor Mere Top, - Buckden Pike	Ingleborough	2050+	625+
220	350	Moel y Cerrig-duon	Arans	2049	625
-	351	Darnbrook Fell, - Fountains Fell	Ingleborough	2048	624
-	352	Fan Frynych, - Rhôs Dringarth	Brecon Beacons	2047	624
221	353	Randygill Top	Great Shunner	2047	624
222	354	Moel Ysgyfarnogod	Rhinogs	2044	623
-	355	Birks, St. Sunday Crag	Helvellyn	2040	622
223	356	Craig-y-llyn	Cader Idris	2040	622
-	357	Higher Shelf Stones, - Bleaklow	Peak District	2039	621
224	358	High Willhays	Dartmoor	2038	621
225	359	Cold Fell	Black Fell	2037	621
226	360	Snaefell	Isle of Man	2036	621
227	361	Bellbeaver Rigg	Cross Fell	2035	620
-	362	Causey Pike, Scar Crags	Buttermere	c. 2035	c. 620
-	363	Long Fell, Little Fell	Cross Fell	2035	620
-	364	Pen y Castell, Drum	Carneddau	2035	620
-	365	Walna Scar, Dow Crag	Coniston	2035	620
-	366	Gallt y Wenallt, - Y Lliwedd	Snowdon	2032	619

228	367	Windy Gyle	Cheviots	2032	619
-	368	Rhos, Foel Wen	Berwyns	2030	619
-	369	Yes Tor, High Willhays	Dartmoor	2030	619
229	370	Bink Moss	Cross Fell	2028	618
-	371	Y Foel, Cadair Bronwen	Berwyns	2028	618
-	372	Bryn-gwyn, Post Gwyn	Berwyns	2025+	617+
-	373	Dovenest Top, - Glaramara	Scafell	2025+	617+
-	374	Sprinkling Crags, - Great End	Scafell	2025+	617+
230	375	Garreg-lwyd	Brecon Beacons	2022	616
231	376	Foel Boeth	Arennigs	2021	616
232	377	Cushat Law	Cheviots	2020	616
233	378	Great Borne	Great Gable	2020	616
-	379	Hartsop Dodd, - Stony Cove Pike	High Street	2018	615
234	380	Drumaldrace	Ingleborough	2015	614
235	381	Flinty Fell	Burnhope Seat	2013	614
236	382	The Dodd	Burnhope Seat	2013	614
-	383	Llechwedd Du, - Foel Rhudd	Arans	2010	613
-	384	Y Gyrn, Pen y Fan	Brecon Beacons	2010	613
237	385	Gorllwyn	Rhayader Mountains	2009	612
-	386	Great Lingy Hill, - High Pike	Skiddaw	2009	612
-	387	Stirrup Crag, Yewbarrow	Great Gable	2009	612
238	388	Foel Goch	Arennigs	2004	611
239	389	Bryn Garw	Rhayader Mountains	2003	611
-	390	Heron Pike, Fairfield	Helvellyn	2003	611
240	391	Pen y Garn Fawr	Black Mountains	2003	611
241	392	Bach Hill	Radnor Forest	2002	610
-	393	Bullman Hills, Cross Fell	Cross Fell	2002	610
242	394	Birks Fell	Ingleborough	2001	610
243	395	Bloodybush Edge	Cheviots	2001	610
244	396	Tal y Fan	Carneddau	2001	610
245	397	Cefn yr Ystrad	Brecon Beacons	2000+	610+
-	398	Foel Goch, Foel y Geifr	Arans	2000+	610+
-	399	Foel Penolau, - Moel Ysgyfarnogod	Rhinogs	2000+	610+
246	400	Middlehope Moor	Burnhope Seat	2000+	610+
-	401	Cefn Gwyntog, - Cyrniau Nôd	Berwyns	2000+	610+
247	402	Moel Pemamnen	Moel Siabod	2000+	610+

-	403	Moel yr Ogof, Moel Lefn	Moel Hebog	2000+	610+
-	404	Pen Cowlyd, - Creigiau Gleision	Carneddau	2000+	610+
-	405	Pen y Cerrig-duon, - Pen y Boncyn trefeilw	Berwyns	2000+	610+
248	406	Pen yr Allt-uchaf	Arans	2000+	610+
-	407	White Maiden, Dow Crag	Coniston	2000+	610+
-	408	Miller Moss, Knott	Skiddaw	2000	610

TABLE 3   MOUNTAINS IN ALPHABETICAL ORDER

(Names not underlined = recommended names; underlined = cross-references, alternative names and summit names;   an asterisk * indicates a separate mountain.)

Mountains and Tops	Group	Page
Allen Crags*	Scafell	54
Allenheads, Middlehope Moor*	Burnhope Seat	72
Allt Fawr*	Moel Siabod	110
Allt Lwyd	Brecon Beacons	142
Amarch, Craig Cwm Amarch	Cader Idris	128
Aran, Yr Aran*	Snowdon	106
Aran Benllyn*	Arans	122
Aran Fawddwy*	Arans	122
Archy Styrigg	Great Shunner	80
Arennig Fach*	Arennigs	116
Arennig Fawr*	Arennigs	116
Artle Crag, Branstree*	High Street	30
Arwystli, Pen Pumlumon Arwystli*	Pumlumon	134
Ashgill Head, Redgleam	Burnhope Seat	72
Auchope Cairn	Cheviots	64
Bach Hill*	Radnor Forest	136
Backstone Edge*	Cross Fell	74
Bannau Brycheiniog*	Brecon Beacons	142
Bannau Sir Gaer*	Brecon Beacons	142
Bannerdale Crags	Skiddaw	42
Base Brown	Great Gable	48
Baugh Fell, Knoutberry Haw*	Great Shunner	80
Bellbeaver Rigg*	Cross Fell	74
Benllyn, Aran Benllyn	Arans	122
Berwyn, Cadair Berwyn	Berwyns	118
Bink Moss*	Cross Fell	74
Birkhouse Moor	Helvellyn	36
Birks	Helvellyn	36
Birks Fell*	Ingleborough	84
Black Fell*	Black Fell	70
Black Fell Moss, Hugh Seat	Great Shunner	82
Black Hill	Burnhope Seat	72
Black Mixen	Radnor Forest	136

Black Mountain*	Black Mountains	146
Black Sails	Coniston	58
Bleaklow*	Peak District	88
Bleaklow Head, Bleaklow*	Peak District	88
Bleaklow Stones, Bleaklow*	Peak District	88
Blencathra*	Skiddaw	42
Bloodybush Edge*	Cheviots	64
Blunt Top	Scafell	54
Boeth, Foel Boeth*	Arennigs	116
Boncyn, Pen y Boncyn trefeilw*	Berwyns	118
Bowfell*	Scafell	54
Bowfell North	Scafell	54
Bowscale Fell*	Skiddaw	42
Bram Rigg Top	Great Shunner	80
Brandreth*	Great Gable	48
Branstree*	High Street	30
Brant Street, Branstree*	High Street	30
Brim Fell	Coniston	58
Broad Crag	Scafell	54
Bronwen, Cadair Bronwen*	Berwyns	118
Brycheiniog, Bannau Brycheiniog*	Brecon Beacons	142
Bryn Garw*	Rhayader Mountains	134
Bryn-gwyn	Berwyns	118
Bryn Teg, Cribin*	Brecon Beacons	142
Buckden Gavel, Buckden Pike*	Ingleborough	84
Buckden Pike*	Ingleborough	84
Bullman Hills	Cross Fell	74
Burnhope Seat*	Burnhope Seat	72
Bwrdd Arthur, Cadair Bronwen*	Berwyns	118
Cadair Berwyn	Berwyns	118
Cadair Bronwen*	Berwyns	118
Cader Idris*	Cader Idris	128
Calders	Great Shunner	80
Calf, The Calf*	Great Shunner	80
Calfhow Pike	Helvellyn	38
Cape, The, St. Sunday Crag*	Helvellyn	36
Carl Side	Skiddaw	42
Carmarthen Van, Bannau Brycheiniog*	Brecon Beacons	142
Carnau'r Gareg Lâs, Gareg Lâs*	Brecon Beacons	142
Carnedd Bochgen, Arennig Fach*	Arennigs	116
Carnedd Dafydd*	Carneddau	100

Carnedd Llechwedd	Arennigs	116
Carnedd Llywelyn*	Carneddau	100
Carnedd Moel Siabod, Moel Siabod*	Moel Siabod	110
Carnedd Penyborth-goch, Drum*	Carneddau	100
Carnedd Ugain, Crib-y-ddysgl*	Snowdon	106
Carnedd y Ddelw	Carneddau	100
Carnedd y Filiast*	Glyders	102
Carnedd y Filiast, Gylchedd*	Arennigs	116
Carrock Fell*	Skiddaw	42
Catchedicam, Catstye Cam*	Helvellyn	36
Catstycam, Catstye Cam*	Helvellyn	36
Catstye Cam*	Helvellyn	36
Caudale Moor, Stony Cove Pike*	High Street	30
Causey Pike	Buttermere	46
Caw Fell	Great Gable	48
Cefn Gwyntog	Berwyns	118
Cefn yr Ystrad*	Brecon Beacons	142
Cerrig-calch, Pen Cerrig-calch*	Black Mountains	146
Cerrig-duon, Moel y Cerrig-duon*	Arans	122
Cerrig-duon, Pen y Cerrig-duon	Berwyns	118
Chapelfell Top*	Burnhope Seat	72
Cheviot, The Cheviot*	Cheviots	64
Chwarel y Fan*	Black Mountains	146
Clough Head*	Helvellyn	38
Cnicht*	Moel Siabod	110
Coldberry End, High Field*	Burnhope Seat	72
Cold Fell*	Black Fell	70
Cold Pike	Scafell	56
Comb Fell*	Cheviots	64
Coniston Old Man, The Old Man of Coniston*	Coniston	58
Corn Dû	Brecon Beacons	142
Crag Hill*	Buttermere	46
Crinkle Crags*	Scafell	54
Craig Cerrig-gleisiad, Rhôs Dringarth*	Brecon Beacons	142
Craig Cwm Amarch	Cader Idris	128
Craig Cwm-du, Foel Hafod-fynydd*	Arans	122
Craig Cwm Silyn*	Moel Hebog	108
Craig-las, Tyrau Mawr*	Cader Idris	128
Craig Lŵyd	Cader Idris	128
Craig-y-llyn*	Cader Idris	128
Creigiau Gleision*	Carneddau	100
Crib-goch*	Snowdon	106

162

Cribin*	Brecon Beacons	142
Cribin Fawr*	Cader Idris	128
Crib-y-ddysgl*	Snowdon	106
Crib-y-rhiw	Rhinogs	126
Cross Fell*	Cross Fell	74
Cushat Law*	Cheviots	64
Cyfrwy	Cader Idris	128
Cyrniau Nôd*	Berwyns	118
Dale Head*	Buttermere	46
Darnbrook Fell	Ingleborough	84
Ddafad-ddu, Erw y Ddafad-ddu	Arans	122
Dduallt, Y Dduallt*	Arennigs	116
Ddysgl, Crib-y-ddysgl*	Snowdon	106
Ddysgl, Trum y Ddysgl*	Moel Hebog	108
Dead Stones	Burnhope Seat	72
Diffwys*	Rhinogs	126
Dodd, The Dodd*	Burnhope Seat	72
Dodd Fell Hill*	Ingleborough	84
Doe Crag, Dow Crag*	Coniston	58
Dollywaggon Pike*	Helvellyn	36
Dove Crag	Helvellyn	36
Dovenest Top	Scafell	54
Dow Crag*	Coniston	58
Drosgl*	Carneddau	100
Drum*	Carneddau	100
Drumaldrace*	Ingleborough	84
Drws-y-coed, Mynydd Drws-y-coed	Moel Hebog	108
Drygarn Fawr*	Rhayader Mountains	134
Dufton Fell, Meldon Hill*	Cross Fell	74
Dun Edge, Melmerby Fell*	Cross Fell	74
Dun Fell, Great Dun Fell* and Little Dun Fell	Cross Fell	74
Duwynt	Brecon Beacons	142
Eel Crag, Crag Hill*	Buttermere	46
Eel Crags, High Spy*	Buttermere	46
Elen, Yr Elen*	Carneddau	100
Elidir Fawr*	Glyders	102
Erw y Ddafad-ddu	Arans	122
Esk Pike*	Scafell	54
Fairfield*	Helvellyn	36
Fan Fawr*	Brecon Beacons	142

Fan Frynych	Brecon Beacons	142
Fan Gihirych*	Brecon Beacons	142
Fan Hir	Brecon Beacons	142
Fan Llia*	Brecon Beacons	142
Fan Nedd*	Brecon Beacons	142
Fawddwy, Aran Fawddwy*	Arans	122
Fell Head*	Great Shunner	80
Fendrith Hill	Burnhope Seat	72
Fiend's Fell*	Cross Fell	74
Filiast, Carnedd y Filiast*	Glyders	102
Filiast, Carnedd y, Gylchedd*	Arennigs	116
Fleetwith Pike*	Great Gable	48
Flesk	Scafell	56
Flinty Fell*	Burnhope Seat	72
Foel, Y Foel	Berwyns	118
Foel Boeth*	Arennigs	116
Foel Cwm-pydew, Trum y Sarn*	Berwyns	118
Foel-fras*	Carneddau	100
Foel Goch	Arans	122
Foel Goch*	Arennigs	116
Foel-goch*	Glyders	102
Foel-grach*	Carneddau	100
Foel-gron	Snowdon	106
Foel Hafod-fynydd*	Arans	122
Foel Hirnant, Foel Goch	Arans	122
Foel Penolau	Rhinogs	126
Foel Rhudd*	Arans	122
Foel Wen*	Berwyns	118
Foel y Geifr*	Arans	122
Foul Moss, Green Hill	Ingleborough	84
Fountains Fell*	Ingleborough	84
Froswick	High Street	30
Fwddog Ridge (Frontier), Chwarel y Fan*	Black Mountains	146
Gadair, Pen y, Cader Idris*	Cader Idris	128
Gader, Pen y, Cader Idris*	Cader Idris	128
Gallt y Daren, Foel Boeth*	Arennigs	116
Gallt yr Ogof	Glyders	102
Gallt y Wenallt	Snowdon	106
Gamblesby Allotments, Fiend's Fell*	Cross Fell	74
Garn, Y Garn*	Glyders	102

Garn, Y Garn	Moel Hebog	108
Garn, Y Garn	Pumlumon	134
Garn, Y Garn*	Rhinogs	126
Garnedd-goch	Moel Hebog	108
Garnedd-uchaf	Carneddau	100
Garreg-lwyd*	Brecon Beacons	142
Geifr, Foel y Geifr*	Arans	122
Glaramara*	Scafell	54
Glasgwm*	Arans	122
Glenridding Common, Birkhouse Moor	Helvellyn	36
Glyder Fâch*	Glyders	102
Glyder Fawr*	Glyders	102
Godor*	Berwyns	118
Gareg Lâs*	Brecon Beacons	142
Gorllwyn*	Rhayader Mountains	134
Gragareth*	Ingleborough	84
Graig Ty-nant, Llechwedd Du	Arans	122
Grasmoor*	Buttermere	46
Great Borne*	Great Gable	50
Great Calva*	Skiddaw	42
Great Carrs	Coniston	54
Great Coum*	Ingleborough	84
Great Creigiau	Radnor Forest	136
Great Dodd*	Helvellyn	38
Great Dun Fell*	Cross Fell	74
Great End*	Scafell	54
Great Gable*	Great Gable	48
Great Knoutberry Hill*	Ingleborough	84
Great Lingy Hill	Skiddaw	42
Great Rhos*	Radnor Forest	136
Great Rigg	Helvellyn	36
Greatrigg Man, Great Rigg	Helvellyn	36
Great Sca Fell	Skiddaw	42
Great Scoat Fell	Great Gable	48
Great Shunner Fell*	Great Shunner	82
Great Whernside*	Ingleborough	86
Green Fell, Knock Fell*	Cross Fell	74
Green Gable	Great Gable	48
Green Hill	Ingleborough	84
Green Side	Helvellyn	38
Gregory Chapel, Archy Styrigg	Great Shunner	80
Grey Crag	High Street	30

Grey Friar*	Coniston	58
Greygarth Hill, Gragareth*	Ingleborough	84
Grey Knotts	Great Gable	48
Grey Nag*	Black Fell	70
Grib-gôch, Crib-gôch*	Snowdon	106
Grisedale Pike*	Buttermere	46
Groes Fagl, Y Groes Fagl	Berwyns	118
Gwaen y Llŵyni	Arans	122
Gwyliwr, Glyder Fach*	Glyders	102
Gylchedd*	Arennigs	116
Gyrn, Y Gyrn	Brecon Beacons	142
Hafod-fynydd, Foel Hafod-fynydd*	Arans	122
Hallsfell Top, Blencathra*	Skiddaw	42
Hangingstone Hill	Cheviots	64
Harrison Stickle	Scafell	54
Hart Crag*	Helvellyn	36
Harter Fell*	Coniston	58
Harter Fell*	High Street	30
Hart Side	Helvellyn	38
Hartsop Dodd	High Street	30
Hay Bluff, Pen y Beacon	Black Mountains	146
Haycock*	Great Gable	48
Hebog, Moel Hebog*	Moel Hebog	108
Hedgehope Hill*	Cheviots	64
Heights, The, Knock Fell*	Cross Fell	74
Helgi-du, Pen yr Helgi-du*	Carneddau	100
Helvellyn*	Helvellyn	36
Herdship Hill, Viewing Hill*	Cross Fell	74
Herdus, Great Borne*	Great Gable	48
Heron Pike	Helvellyn	36
High Crag*	Great Gable	48
High Crag	Helvellyn	36
Higher Shelf Stones	Peak District	88
High Field*	Burnhope Seat	72
High Pike*	Skiddaw	42
High Raise*	High Street	30
High Raise*	Scafell	54
High Seat*	Great Shunner	80
High Spy*	Buttermere	46
High Spying How, Striding Edge	Helvellyn	36

High Stile*	Great Gable	48
High Street*	High Street	30
High White Stones, High Raise*	Scafell	54
High Willhays*	Dartmoor	92
High Willes, High Willhays*	Dartmoor	92
Hilton Fell, Little Fell*	Cross Fell	74
Hindscarth*	Buttermere	46
Hirnant, Foel, Foel Goch	Arans	122
Hobcarton Pike, Hopegill Head*	Buttermere	46
Hopegill Head*	Buttermere	46
Hudeshope Fell, James's Hill*	Burnhope Seat	72
Hugh Seat	Great Shunner	82
Ill Bell, Kentmere*	High Street	30
Ill Bell, Mardale Ill Bell	High Street	30
Ill Crag	Scafell	54
Ingleborough Hill*	Ingleborough	84
Iron Crag*	Great Gable	48
James's Hill*	Burnhope Seat	72
John Bell's Banner, Stony Cove Pike*	High Street	30
Kentmere, Ill Bell, Kentmere*	High Street	30
Kentmere Pike	High Street	30
Killhope Law*	Burnhope Seat	72
Kilnshaw Chimney*	Helvellyn	36
Kinder Scout*	Peak District	88
Kirk Fell East	Great Gable	48
Kirk Fell West*	Great Gable	48
Knock Fell*	Cross Fell	74
Knott*	Skiddaw	42
Knott, The Knott	High Street	30
Knoutberry Haw*	Great Shunner	72
Ladyside Pike	Buttermere	46
Lady's Seat, Ladyside Pike	Buttermere	46
Lincombe Tarns	Scafell	54
Lingmell*	Scafell	54
Little Dun Fell	Cross Fell	74
Little Fell*	Cross Fell	74
Little Hart Crag	Helvellyn	36

Little Man	Skiddaw	42
Little Scoat Fell*	Great Gable	48
Little Walls, Wetherlam*	Coniston	58
Llechog*	Snowdon	106
Llechwedd, Carnedd Llechwedd	Arennigs	116
Llechwedd, Moel Llechwedd	Arennigs	116
Llechwedd Du	Arans	122
Llethr, Y Llethr*	Rhinogs	126
Llithrig y Wrâch, Pen Llithrig y Wrâch*	Carneddau	100
Lliwedd, Y Lliwedd*	Snowdon	102
Llwytmor	Carneddau	100
Llyfnant, Moel Llyfnant*	Arennigs	116
Llygad-bychan, Pen Pumlumon Llygad-bychan*	Pumlumon	134
Llysiau, Mynydd Llysiau	Black Mountains	146
Loadpot Hill	High Street	30
Lobstone Band, High Spy*	Buttermere	46
Loft Crag	Scafell	56
Long Crag	Cross Fell	74
Long Fell	Cross Fell	74
Long Man Hill	Cross Fell	74
Long Side	Skiddaw	42
Lonscale Fell*	Skiddaw	42
Looking Stead	Great Gable	48
Looking Stead	Scafell	54
Lord Hereford's Knob, The Tumpa*	Black Mountains	146
Lovely Seat*	Great Shunner	82
Lower Man	Helvellyn	36
Low Man, Little Man	Skiddaw	42
Maen Du, Maesglasau*	Cader Idris	128
Maesglasau*	Cader Idris	128
Maes-glase, Maesglasau*	Cader Idris	128
Manod Mawr North	Moel Siabod	110
Manod Mawr South*	Moel Siabod	110
Mardale Ill Bell	High Street	30
Meldon Hill*	Cross Fell	74
Melmerby Fell*	Cross Fell	74
Mickle Fell*	Cross Fell	74
Middle Currick, Grey Nag*	Black Fell	70
Middlehope Moor*	Burnhope Seat	72
Middle Scoat Fell	Great Gable	48

Milburn Forest, Great Dun Fell* and Little Dun Fell	Cross Fell	74
Miller Moss	Skiddaw	42
Moel Bleiddiau, Ysgafell Wen*	Moel Siabod	110
Moel Druman	Moel Siabod	110
Moel Eilio*	Snowdon	106
Moel Fferna*	Berwyns	118
Moel Gornach, Garreg-Lwyd*	Brecon Beacons	142
Moel Hebog*	Moel Hebog	108
Moel Lefn*	Moel Hebog	108
Moel Llechwedd	Arennigs	116
Moel Llyfnant*	Arennigs	116
Moel Nant yr Ogof*	Glyders	102
Moel Penamnen*	Moel Siabod	110
Moel Poethion*	Berwyns	118
Moel Siabod*	Moel Siabod	110
Moel Sych*	Berwyns	118
Moelwyn Bach*	Moel Siabod	110
Moelwyn Mawr*	Moel Siabod	110
Moel y Cerrig-duon*	Arans	122
Moel y Cynghorion*	Snowdon	106
Moel yr Eglwys, Arennig Fawr*	Arennigs	116
Moel-yr-hydd*	Moel Siabod	110
Moel yr Ogof	Moel Hebog	108
Moel Ysgyfarnogod*	Rhinogs	126
Mosedale Pike, Nowtli Hill	High Street	30
Murton Fell*	Cross Fell	74
Mynydd Carnedd Hywel, Foel y Geifr*	Arans	122
Mynydd Drws-y-coed	Moel Hebog	108
Mynydd Gwerngraig	Cader Idris	128
Mynydd Llangynidr, Cefn yr Ystrad*	Brecon Beacons	142
Mynydd Llysiau	Black Mountains	146
Mynydd Mawr*	Moel Hebog	108
Mynydd Moel*	Cader Idris	128
Mynydd Pencoed	Cader Idris	128
Mynydd Perfedd	Glyders	102
Mynydd Tal-y-mignedd*	Moel Hebog	108
Mynydd Tarw	Berwyns	118
Nethermost Pike	Helvellyn	36
Nine Standards Rigg	Great Shunner	80
Nowtli Hill	High Street	30

Ogof, Gallt yr Ogof	Glyders	102
Ogof, Moel Nant yr Ogof*	Glyders	102
Ogof, Moel yr Ogof	Moel Hebog	108
Old Man of Coniston, The,*	Coniston	58
Oleu-wen, Pen-yr-oleu-wen*	Carneddau	100
Outberry Plain	Burnhope Seat	72
Pen Allt-mawr*	Black Mountains	146
Pen-aran	Arans	122
Pen Cerrig-calch*	Black Mountains	146
Pencoed, Mynydd Pencoed	Cader Idris	128
Pen Cowlyd	Carneddau	100
Pen Llithrig y Wrach*	Carneddau	100
Penolau, Foel Penolau	Rhinogs	126
Pen Pumlumon Arwystli*	Pumlumon	134
Pen Pumlumon Fawr*	Pumlumon	134
Pen Pumlumon Llygad-bychan*	Pumlumon	134
Pen-twyn-mawr	Black Mountains	146
Pen y Beacon	Black Mountains	146
Pen y Boncyn trefeilw*	Berwyns	118
Pen-y-bryn	Berwyns	118
Pen y Bryn-fforchog	Arans	122
Pen y Castell	Carneddau	100
Pen y Cerrig-duon	Berwyns	118
Pen y Diocyn	Arennigs	116
Pen y Fan*	Brecon Beacons	142
Pen y Gadair, Cader Idris*	Cader Idris	128
Pen y Gader-Fawr	Black Mountains	146
Pen y Garw, Bryn Garw*	Rhayader Mountains	134
Pen y Garn Fawr*	Black Mountains	146
Penyghent Hill*	Ingleborough	84
Pen y Gorllwyn, Gorllwyn*	Rhayader Mountains	134
Pen yr Allt-uchaf*	Arans	122
Pen yr Helgi-du*	Carneddau	100
Pen-yr-oleu-wen*	Carneddau	100
Picws Du, Bannau Sir Gaer*	Brecon Beacons	142
Pike o' Blisco*	Scafell	56
Pike o' Stickle	Scafell	54
Pillar Fell*	Great Gable	48
Pillar Rock	Great Gable	48
Place Fell*	High Street	30

Plover Hill*	Ingleborough	84
Plynlimon, Pumlumon Group	Pumlumon	134
Poethion, Moel Poethion*	Berwyns	118
Post Gwyn*	Berwyns	118
Pydew, Foel Cwm-pydew, Trum y Sarn*	Berwyns	118
Raise*	Helvellyn	36
Raise, High Raise*	High Street	30
Raise, High Raise*	Scafell	54
Ramsgill Head, Rampsgill Head	High Street	30
Rampsgill Head,	High Street	30
Ramsden Pike, Buckden Pike*	Ingleborough	84
Randygill Top*	Great Shunner	80
Raven Crag, Kentmere Pike	High Street	30
Redgleam	Burnhope Seat	72
Red Pike, Ennerdale*	Great Gable	48
Red Pike, Wasdale*	Great Gable	48
Red Screes, Kilnshaw Chimney*	Helvellyn	36
Rest Dodd*	High Street	30
Rhinog Fach*	Rhinogs	126
Rhinog Fawr*	Rhinogs	126
Rhobell Fawr*	Arennigs	116
Rhos	Berwyns	118
Rhos Dirion	Black Mountains	146
Rhôs Dringarth*	Brecon Beacons	142
Robinson*	Buttermere	46
Rogan's Seat*	Great Shunner	80
Rossett Pike	Scafell	54
Rough Crag	High Seat	30
Round Hill*	Cross Fell	74
Russell's Cairn, Windy Gyle*	Cheviots	64
Saddleback, Blencathra*	Skiddaw	42
Saddle, The, Cyfrwy	Cader Idris	128
Sail	Buttermere	46
Sails*	Great Shunner	82
Sails, Black Sails	Coniston	58
St. Sunday Crag*	Helvellyn	36
Sale How	Skiddaw	42
Scafell*	Scafell	54
Scafell Pike*	Scafell	54
Scar Crags*	Buttermere	46

<u>Scawdel Fell</u>, High Spy*	Buttermere	46
<u>Scoat Fell</u>, Great Scoat Fell, Little Scoat Fell* and Middle Scoat Fell	Great Gable	48
Seatallan*	Great Gable	48
<u>Seathwaite Fell</u>, Sprinkling Crags	Scafell	54
Seat Sandal*	Helvellyn	36
Selside Pike	High Street	30
Sheffield Pike*	Helvellyn	38
Shelter Crags	Scafell	56
<u>Shunner</u>, Great Shunner Fell*	Great Shunner	80
<u>Silyn</u>, Craig Cwm Silyn*	Moel Hebog	108
Simon Fell	Ingleborough	84
Simon Fell North	Ingleborough	84
Skiddaw*	Skiddaw	42
<u>Skiddaw Man</u>, Skiddaw*	Skiddaw	42
Slight Side	Scafell	54
Snaefell	Isle of Man	94
<u>Snowdon</u>, Y Wyddfa*	Snowdon	106
Sprinkling Crags	Scafell	54
<u>Spying How, High</u>, Striding Edge	Helvellyn	36
Stac Rhôs	Berwyns	118
Stangend Rigg	Burnhope Seat	72
<u>Starbottom Out Moor</u>, Tor Mere Top	Ingleborough	84
Starling Dodd	Great Gable	50
Steeple	Great Gable	48
Stirrup Crag	Great Gable	48
Stony Cove Pike*	High Street	30
St. Sunday Crag*	Helvellyn	36
Striding Edge	Helvellyn	36
Stybarrow Dod*	Helvellyn	36
Swarth Fell*	Great Shunner	80
Swarth Fell Pike	Great Shunner	80
Swirl How*	Coniston	58
Tal y Fan*	Carneddau	100
<u>Tal-y-mignedd</u>, Mynydd Tal-y-mignedd	Moel Hebog	108
Tarn Crag*	High Street	30
Tarn Crags Top	Skiddaw	42
Tarn Rigg Hill	Great Shunner	80
Tarrenhendre*	Cader Idris	128
Tarren y Gesail*	Cader Idris	128

The Calf*	Great Shunner	80
The Cape, St. Sunday Crag*	Helvellyn	36
The Cheviot*	Cheviots	64
The Dodd*	Burnhope Seat	72
The Heights, Knock Fell*	Cross Fell	74
The Knott	High Street	30
The Old Man of Coniston*	Coniston	58
The Saddle, Cyfrwy	Cader Idris	128
The Tumpa*	Black Mountains	146
Thornhope Carrs, Grey Nag*	Black Fell	70
Thornthwaite Beacon, Thornthwaite Crag	High Street	30
Thornthwaite Crag	High Street	30
Three Pikes	Burnhope Seat	72
Thunacarr Knott	Scafell	54
Tomle	Berwyns	118
Tor Mere Top	Ingleborough	84
Trum y Ddysgl*	Moel Hebog	108
Trum y Sarn*	Berwyns	118
Tryfan*	Glyders	102
Tumpa, The Tumpa*	Black Mountains	146
Tyrau Mawr*	Cader Idris	128
Ullock Pike	Skiddaw	42
Ullscarf*	Scafell	56
Ure Head, Sails*	Great Shunner	80
Viewing Hill*	Cross Fell	74
Waen-rydd*	Brecon Beacons	142
Walna Scar	Coniston	58
Wandope, Wanlope	Buttermere	46
Wanlope	Buttermere	46
Water Crag	Great Shunner	80
Waun Fach*	Black Mountains	146
Waun-oer*	Cader Idris	128
Weather Hill, Wether Hill*	High Street	30
Westernhope Moor, James's Hill*	Burnhope Seat	72
Wether Fell, Drumaldrace*	Ingleborough	84
Wether Hill*	High Street	30
Wetherlam*	Coniston	58
Whernside*	Ingleborough	84
Whernside, Great Whernside*	Ingleborough	86

Whiteless Pike	Buttermere	46
White Maiden	Coniston	58
White Mossy Hill*	Great Shunner	80
White Pike, Clough Head*	Helvellyn	36
Whiteside*	Buttermere	46
White Side	Helvellyn	36
Whiteside Bank, White Side	Helvellyn	36
White Stones, Green Side	Helvellyn	38
Widdale Fell, Great Knoutberry Hill*	Ingleborough	84
Wild Boar Fell*	Great Shunner	80
Windygate Hill, Windy Gyle*	Cheviots	64
Windy Gyle*	Cheviots	64
Wyddfa, Y Wyddfa*	Snowdon	106
Yarlside*	Great Shunner	80
Y Dduallt*	Arennigs	116
Yes Tor	Dartmoor	92
Yewbarrow*	Great Gable	48
Y Foel	Berwyns	118
Y Garn*	Glyders	102
Y Garn	Moel Hebog	108
Y Garn	Pumlumon	134
Y Garn*	Rhinogs	126
Y Groes Fagl	Berwyns	118
Y Gyrn	Brecon Beacons	142
Y Llethr*	Rhinogs	126
Y Lliwedd*	Snowdon	106
Yockenthwaite Moor*	Ingleborough	84
Yoke	High Street	30
Yolk, Yoke	High Street	30
Yr Aran*	Snowdon	106
Yr Elen*	Carneddau	100
Yr Wyddfa, Y Wyddfa*	Snowdon	106
Ysgafell Wen*	Moel Siabod	110
Ysgyfarnogod, Moel Ysgyfarnogod*	Rhinogs	126
Ystrad, Cefn yr Ystrad*	Brecon Beacons	142
Y Wyddfa*	Snowdon	106

TABLE 4   COUNTY TOPS OF ENGLAND AND WALES

The Notes to Table 1 apply generally here also.   As rather more of these tops lie on private land than those listed in the other Tables, the remarks made there about access are even more relevant here, and would-be visitors should tread circumspectly, and remember that the friendly approach pays the greatest dividends.   As pointed out before, information given in this book should not be taken as evidence of a right of way.

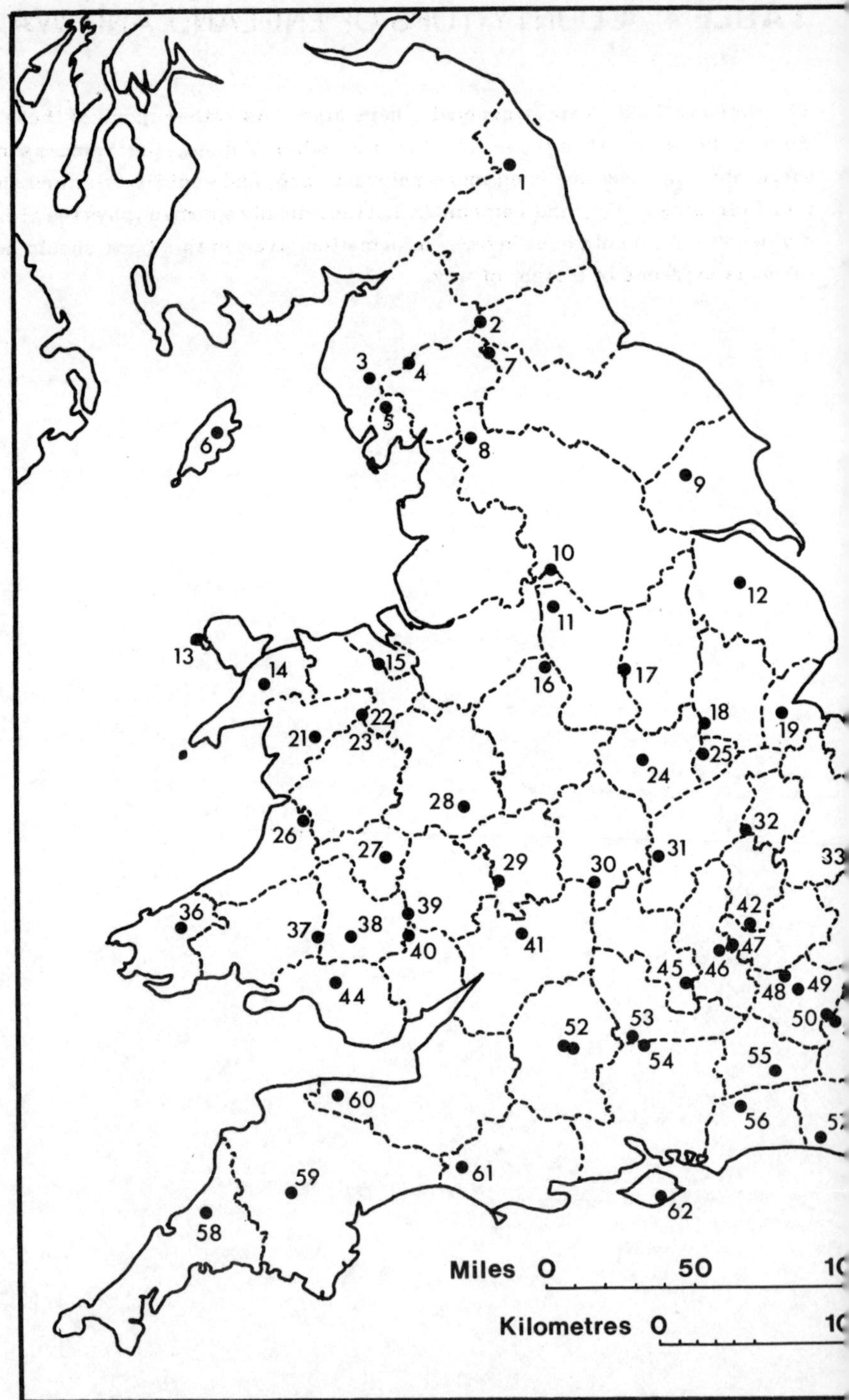
Miles 0   50   10
Kilometres 0   10

1 Northumberland
2 Durham
3 Cumberland
4 Westmorland
5 Lancashire
6 Isle of Man
7 Yorkshire, North Riding
8 Yorkshire, West Riding
9 Yorkshire, East Riding
10 Cheshire
11 Derbyshire
12 Lincolnshire, Lindsey
13 Anglesey
14 Caernarvonshire
15 Flintshire
16 Staffordshire
17 Nottinghamshire
18 Lincolnshire, Kesteven
19 Lincolnshire, Holland
20 Norfolk
21 Merionethshire
22 Denbighshire
23 Montgomeryshire
24 Leicestershire
25 Rutlandshire
26 Cardiganshire
27 Radnorshire
28 Shropshire
29 Worcestershire
30 Warwickshire
31 Northamptonshire

32 Huntingdonshire
33 Cambridgeshire
34 Suffolk, West
35 Suffolk, East
36 Pembrokeshire
37 Carmarthenshire
38 Brecknockshire
39 Herefordshire
40 Monmouthshire
41 Gloucestershire
42 Hertfordshire
43 Essex
44 Glamorgan
45 Oxfordshire
46 Buckinghamshire
47 Bedfordshire
48 Middlesex
49 London (old county)
50 Greater London
51 Kent
52 Wiltshire
53 Berkshire
54 Hampshire
55 Surrey
56 Sussex, West
57 Sussex, East
58 Cornwall
59 Devon
60 Somerset
61 Dorset
62 Isle of Wight

THE COUNTY TOPS
OF ENGLAND AND WALES

County	Name	Height feet	metres	Maps 1" 2½" T	Grid Ref.
Anglesey	Holyhead Mountain[1]	722[2]	220	106 SH28 T	218829
Bedfordshire[3]	Dunstable Downs	801	244	147 TL01	c.008194
Berkshire[4]	Walbury Hill	974	297	168 SU36	373616
Brecknockshire	Pen y Fan	2906	886	141 SO02	012215
Buckinghamshire[5]	Wendover Woods[6]	857	261	159 SP80	897085
Caernarvonshire	Y Wyddfa (Snowdon)	3560*	1085	106 SH65 T[7] 107	609544
Cambridgeshire[8]	Point 480	480	146	148 TL43 T[9]	427380
Cardiganshire	Pen Pumlumon Fawr	2468*	752	127 SN78	789869
Carmarthenshire	Fan Foel	2500+[10]	762+	140 SN82	820223
Cheshire[11]	Black Hill (summit = Soldiers Lump)	1908	582	102 SE00 T[12]	078046
Cornwall	Brown Willy	1377	420	186 SX17	158799
Cumberland[13]	Scafell Pike	3210*	978	82 NY20 T[14]	215072
Denbighshire[15]	Moel Sych	2713*	827	117 SJ03	066318
Derbyshire[16]	Kinder Scout	2088*	636	102 SK08 T[17] 111	086875
Devon	High Willhays	2038*	621	175 SX48/58 T[18]	579891
Dorset	Pilsdon Pen	908	277	177 ST40	413011
Durham[19]	Point 2449 on Burn-hope Seat	2449	746	84 NY73	787375
Essex[20]	Chishall Common	458	140	148 TL43 T[21]	433362
Flintshire	Moel Fammau	1817	555	108 SJ16	161626
Glamorgan	Pen y Craig-y-llyn[22]	1969	600	154 SN90	906031
Gloucestershire	Cleeve Cloud	1082	330	143 SO92 144	996245
Hampshire[23]	Pilot Hill	937	286	168 SU36	398601
Herefordshire[24]	Black Mountain	2306*	703	141 SO23	255350

Position	Best Ascended From	County Top No. in order of Altitude	Asc-ended
$1\frac{3}{4}$ mi. W of Holyhead	Unclassified road, $\frac{1}{2}$ mi. to S	49	
$1\frac{1}{2}$ mi. SSW of Dunstable	B. 4541 nearby	46	
10 mi. N of Andover	Unclassified road to N	31	
5 mi. SSW of Brecon	Nant Gwdi, $2\frac{1}{2}$ mi. to NNE	5	
$1\frac{3}{4}$ mi. E of Wendover	Point 857 is a spot height on an unclassified road	38	
4 mi. SE of Llanberis	Pen-y-pass (Gorphwysfa), $2\frac{1}{2}$ mi. to ENE, see also Table 1, p.	1	
$4\frac{1}{2}$ mi. ESE of Royston; just 300 yds S of The Hall, Great Chishill village	Great Chishill village	54	
9 mi. SSE of Machynllcth	Nant-y-moch Reservoir dam, 2 mi. to WSW	12	
8 mi. SSE of Llandovery	Llanddeusant, 3 mi. to NW	11	
7 mi. NE of Glossop	A. 6024 road, $1\frac{1}{4}$ mi. to SE	22	
$9\frac{1}{2}$ mi. NE of Bodmin	Unclassified road at Cadda, $1\frac{3}{4}$ mi. to SE	29	
2 mi. E of Wastwater	Wasdale Head, 2 mi. to NW	2	
7 mi. S of Corwen	Tan-y-pistyll, $1\frac{1}{2}$ mi. to SSW	6	
3 mi. E of Hayfield	Upper Booth, Edale, $1\frac{3}{4}$ mi. to SSE	18	
$3\frac{1}{2}$ mi. S of Okehampton	Unclassified road 1 mi. to E	19	
$7\frac{1}{2}$ mi. ENE of Axminster	B. 3164 road, 200 yds to S	37	
$7\frac{1}{4}$ mi. SE of Alston	Darngill Bridge, $\frac{3}{4}$ mi. to WSW	13	
$6\frac{1}{2}$ mi. WSW of Saffron Walden	Point 458 is a spot height on an unclassified road	55	
$4\frac{3}{4}$ mi. W of Mold	Unclassified road, $1\frac{1}{4}$ mi. to S	23	
6 mi. W of Aberdare	A. 4061 road, 1 mi. to E	21	
3 mi. ENE of Gloucester	Unclassified road, $\frac{1}{4}$ mi. to NW	30	
$9\frac{1}{2}$ mi. NNE of Andover	Unclassified road, $\frac{1}{2}$ mi. to E	34	
5 mi. SSE of Hay-on-Wye	Unclassified road, 1 mi. to W	15	

Hertfordshire[25]	Point 802	802	244	159 SP90	914091
Huntingdonshire	Point 266	266	81	134 TL07	049713
Isle of Man[26]	Snaefell	2036*	621	87 SC38	397880
Isle of Wight	St. Boniface Down	785	239	180 SZ57	565784
Kent[28]	Betsom's Hill	824	251	171 TQ45 T[29]	435563
Lancashire[30]	The Old Man of Coniston	2631*	802	88 SD29 T[31]	272978
Leicestershire	Bardon Hill	912	278	121 SK41	459131 and 461131
Lincolnshire, Parts of Holland	Pinchbeck Marsh	25	8	123 TF22	263276
Lincolnshire, Parts of Kesteven[32]	500-foot contour	500	152	122 SK82	889232
Lincolnshire, Parts of Lindsey	Point 550	550	168	104 TF19	120964
London, Greater[33]	Point near Hawley's Corner	809	247	171 TQ45 T[34]	c.435565
London[35]	Hampstead Heath	441[36]	134	160 TQ28 T[34]	264867
Merionethshire	Aran Fawddwy	2974*	906	116 SH82 T[37]	862223
Middlesex[38]	Bushey Heath	506[39]	154	160 TQ19 T[40]	153939
Monmouthshire[41]	Chwarel y Fan	2228*	679	141 SO22	259294
Montgomeryshire[42]	Moel Sych	2713*	827	117 SJ03	066318
Norfolk	Roman Camp	336	102	126 TG14	c.185415
Northamptonshire	Arbury Hill	734	224	132 SP55	539587
Northumberland	The Cheviot	2674*	815	71 NT92	909205
Nottinghamshire	Herrod's Hill	655[43]	200	112 SK45	c.467597
Oxfordshire[44]	Shirburn Hill	835	255	159 SU79	723952
Pembrokeshire	Foel-cwmcerwyn	1760	536	139 SN03	093311
Radnorshire	Great Rhos	2166*	660	128 SO06	182638

$1\frac{1}{2}$ mi. SSW of Tring	Point is spot height on unclassified road	45
$6\frac{1}{4}$ mi. ENE of Rushden	Point is near old bridge on farm track, $\frac{1}{2}$ mi. NW of Covington village	59
3 mi. NW of Laxey	Bungalow Station, $\frac{3}{4}$ mi. to S	20
$\frac{1}{2}$ mi. N of Ventnor	Ventnor, $\frac{1}{2}$ mi. to S [27]	47
$1\frac{3}{4}$ mi. SE of Biggin Hill	A. 233 road, 200 yds to NE	41
$1\frac{3}{4}$ mi. W of Coniston	Coniston, $1\frac{3}{4}$ mi. to E	9
2 mi. E of Coalville	Point on A. 50, nearly 1 mi. to S	36
3 mi. NNE of Spalding	Unclassified road, 220 yds to SW	60
$7\frac{3}{4}$ mi. SSW of Grantham	Unclassified road crossing 500-foot contour at county boundary	53
$4\frac{1}{2}$ mi. N of Market Rasen	Unclassified roads 500 yds to W and S	52
$1\frac{1}{2}$ mi. SE of Biggin Hill; 33 yds SE of "Westerham Heights", a house on county boundary.	A. 233 road	43
$2\frac{1}{4}$ mi. NNW of Regent's Park, London	Spot Height on B-class road	-
$4\frac{1}{2}$ mi. N of Dinas Mawddwy	Blaen-pennant, $2\frac{1}{2}$ mi. to E	4
1 mi. SE of Bushey	A. 409 road nearby. Area is much disturbed and built-up	-
7 mi. ESE of Talgarth	Llanthony, 2 mi. to SE	16
7 mi. S of Corwen	Tan-y-pistyll, $1\frac{1}{2}$ mi. to SSW	7
$1\frac{1}{4}$ mi. S of Sheringham	A. 148 road a few yards to N	57
3 mi. SW of Daventry	Unclassified road 100 yds to N	48
7 mi. SW of Wooler	Longleeford, $2\frac{1}{2}$ mi. to ENE	8
$4\frac{1}{2}$ mi. WSW of Mansfield	Huthwaite Sutton in Ashfield. Top is in a built-up area	50
$6\frac{1}{2}$ mi. S of Thame	Unclassified road to E	40
$10\frac{1}{2}$ mi. SSW of Cardigan	Unclassified road, $1\frac{1}{4}$ mi. to SSE	25
$7\frac{1}{2}$ mi. ENE of Llandrindod Wells	New Radnor, $2\frac{1}{2}$ mi. to SE	17

Rutland[45]	Cold Overton Park	646	197	122 SK80	827085
Shropshire	Abdon Burf (Brown Clee Hill)	1772	540	129 SO58	593865
Somerset	Dunkery Beacon	1705	520	164 ST84 T[46]	891415
Staffordshire[47]	Oliver Hill	1684	513	111 SK06 T[48]	027675
Suffolk, East	Wattisham Airfield	300+	91+	149 TM05	029512
Suffolk, West	Elms Farm, Deepden	419	128	149 TL75	786558
Surrey	Leith Hill[49]	965	294	170 TQ14	139431
Sussex, East	Ditchling Beacon	813	248	182 TQ21/31	331130
Sussex, West	Black Down	919	280	181 SU92	919296
Warwickshire	Point 854	854	260	144 SP14	187425
Westmorland[50]	Helvellyn	3116*	949	83 NY31 T[51]	341151
Wiltshire	Milk Hill and Tan Hill[52]	964 964	294 294	167 SU16	104641 081646
Worcestershire	Worcestershire Beacon	1394	425	143 SO74 T[53]	768452
Yorkshire, East Riding	Bishop Wilton Wold	807	246	98 SE95	820569
Yorkshire, North Riding[54]	Mickle Fell (DANGER - see note on page)	2591*	790	84 NY82	805245
Yorkshire, West Riding	Whernside	2419*	737	90 SD78	738814

8 mi. SE of Melton Mowbray	Unclassified road, $\frac{1}{4}$ mi. to N	51
8$\frac{1}{2}$ mi. S of Much Wenlock	Unclassified road, $\frac{3}{4}$ mi. to NE	24
5$\frac{1}{2}$ mi. SW of Minehead	Unclassified road, $\frac{1}{2}$ mi. to E	26
4 mi. SSW of Buxton	Unclassified road 220 yds to SE	27
11$\frac{1}{2}$ mi. NE of Sudbury	Wattisham Airfield. 300-foot contour ring among the buildings	58
10$\frac{1}{2}$ mi. NW of Sudbury	A. 143 road, $\frac{1}{2}$ mi. to NW	56
4$\frac{1}{2}$ mi. SW of Dorking	Unclassified road about 200 yds to SE	32
5$\frac{1}{2}$ mi. N of Brighton	Unclassified road a few hundred yds to E	42
2$\frac{1}{4}$ mi. SSE of Haslemere	Unclassified road, $\frac{1}{2}$ mi. to E	35
Near Hidcote Bartrim, 7$\frac{3}{4}$ mi. S of Stratford-upon-Avon	Unclassified road, $\frac{1}{4}$ mi. to S	39
3$\frac{1}{2}$ mi. W of Patterdale	Thirlspot, 2 mi. to NW; but see also Table 1, p	3
5 and 6$\frac{1}{4}$ mi. ENE of Devizes	Unclassified roads, $\frac{3}{4}$ mi. to E and 1 mi. to S respectively	33
$\frac{1}{2}$ mi. SW of Great Malvern	A. 449 road, $\frac{1}{2}$ mi. to NE	28
13 mi. E of York	A. 166 road, immediately to S	44
6 mi. N of Brough	Langdon Beck, 5 mi. to NNE	10
9$\frac{1}{2}$ mi. SW of Hawes	Unclassified road, 1 mi. to W	14

[1] Anglesey.   At the summit is the feature Caer y Twr.

[2] Anglesey.   Snowdonia National Park Half-inch Tourist Map.

[3] Bedfordshire.   Buckinghamshire and Hertfordshire County Tops are about 10 miles to SW.

[4] Berkshire.   Hampshire County Top is $1\frac{3}{4}$ miles to SE.

[5] Buckinghamshire.   Hertfordshire County Top is $1\frac{1}{4}$ miles to ENE; Bedfordshire C.T. is 10 miles to NE; and Oxfordshire C.T. is $13\frac{1}{2}$ miles to SW.

[6] Buckinghamshire.   Also: "Haddington Hill" (E. Moss).

[7] Caernarvonshire.   Snowdonia National Park Half-inch Tourist Map.

[8] Cambridgeshire.   Essex County Top is $1\frac{1}{2}$ miles to S.

[9] Cambridgeshire.   Cambridge One-inch Tourist Map.

[10] Carmarthenshire.   The highest point on the county boundary. Fan Foel is a spur of Bannau Brycheiniog, Carmarthen Van, which is, as it happens, situated in Brecknockshire.

[11] Cheshire.   Derbyshire County Top is $10\frac{1}{2}$ miles to S.

[12] Cheshire.   Peak District One-inch Tourist Map.

[13] Cumberland.   Lancashire County Top is $6\frac{3}{4}$ miles to SE; Westmorland C.T. is $9\frac{1}{4}$ miles to NE.   See also note to this peak in Table 1.

[14] Cumberland.   Lake District One-inch Tourist Map.

[15] Denbighshire.   Montgomeryshire shares the same County Top.

[16] Derbyshire.   Cheshire County Top is $10\frac{1}{2}$ miles to N; Staffordshire C.T. is 13 miles to SSW.

[17] Derbyshire.   Peak District One-inch Tourist Map.

[18] Devon.   Dartmoor One-inch Tourist Map.

[19] Durham.   Yorkshire, North Riding County Top is 8 miles to S.

[20] Essex.   Cambridgeshire County Top is $1\frac{1}{2}$ miles to N.

[21] Essex.   Cambridge One-inch Tourist Map.

[22] Glamorgan.   Author's temporary name.   From Craig y Llyn, $\frac{1}{4}$ mile to NE. of summit.

[23] Hampshire.   Berkshire County Top is $1\frac{3}{4}$ miles to NW.

[24] Herefordshire.   Monmouthshire County Top is $3\frac{1}{2}$ miles to S.

[25] Hertfordshire.   Buckinghamshire County Top is $1\frac{1}{4}$ miles to WSW; Bedfordshire C.T. is 9 miles to NE; and Oxfordshire C.T. is $14\frac{1}{2}$ miles to SW.

[26] Isle of Man.   Not strictly a county at all, of course.   See also notes to Snaefell in Table 1 (p   ).

[27] Isle of Wight.   Access cannot be guaranteed to this top.

[28] Kent.   Greater London County Top is only 200-odd yards to N.

[29]Kent.   Greater London One-inch Tourist Map.

[30]Lancashire.   Cumberland County Top is $6\frac{3}{4}$ miles to NW;   Westmorland C.T. is $11\frac{1}{2}$ miles to NNE.

[31]Lancashire.   Lake District One-inch Tourist Map.

[32]Lincolnshire, Parts of Kesteven. Rutland County Top is $9\frac{1}{2}$ miles to SSW.

[33]London, Greater.   Kent County Top is only 200-odd yards to S.

[34]London, Greater.   Greater London One-inch Tourist Map.

[35]London.   The old county, now absorbed into Greater London along with parts of several of the surrounding counties and all of Middlesex.

[36]London.   441 (E. Moss's list).

[37]Merionethshire.   Snowdonia National Park Half-inch Tourist Map.

[38]Middlesex.   Now absorbed in Greater London.

[39]Middlesex.   506 (E. Moss's list).

[40]Middlesex.   Greater London One-inch Tourist Map.

[41]Monmouthshire.   Herefordshire County Top is $3\frac{1}{2}$ miles to N.

[42]Montgomeryshire.   Denbighshire shares the same County Top.

[43]Nottinghamshire.   Six-inch Map.

[44]Oxfordshire.   Buckinghamshire and Hertfordshire County Tops are about 14 miles to NE.

[45]Rutland.   Lincolnshire, Parts of Kesteven, County Top is about $9\frac{1}{2}$ miles to NNE.

[46]Somerset.   Exmoor One-inch Tourist Map.

[47]Staffordshire.   Derbyshire County Top is 13 miles to NNE.

[48]Staffordshire.   Peak District One-inch Tourist Map.

[49]Surrey.   The tower was built on the summit to achieve an altitude of 1000 feet.

[50]Westmorland.   Cumberland County Top is $9\frac{1}{4}$ miles to SW;   Lancashire C.T. is is $11\frac{1}{2}$ miles to SSW.   See note to this peak in Table 1.

[51]Westmorland.   Lake District One-inch Tourist Map.

[52]Wiltshire.   Two summits about $1\frac{1}{2}$ miles apart on the same ridge.

[53]Worcestershire.   Wye Valley and Lower Severn One-inch Tourist Map.

[54]Yorkshire, North Riding.   Durham County Top is 8 miles to N.

BIBLIOGRAPHY

*works consulted

Blackshaw, Alan, <u>Mountaineering: From Hill Walking to Alpine Climbing</u>, Penguin Books, 1970. The best handbook for all aspects of mountaineering sport and travel. Excellent bibliography and a long list of addresses of relevant organisations.

British Mountaineering Council; Room 314, 26 Park Crescent, London, WIN 4EE. Various publications including magazine "Mountain Life", Yearbook, and technical circulars on equipment and safety.

Byne, Eric, <u>High Peak: The Story of Walking and Climbing in The Peak</u> District, Secker & Warburg, 1966.

Carr, H.R.C., and Lister, G.A., <u>The Mountains of Snowdonia</u>, Crosby Lockwood & Son Ltd., 1925 and 1948.

Condry, W.M., <u>The Snowdonia National Park</u>, Collins New Naturalist Series, 1969.

Countryside Commission; 1 Cambridge Gate, Regent's Park, London, NW1 4JY. Various publications of interest to all outdoor people, including <u>Countryside Information Directory</u>, an annotated list of organisations having interests in the countryside. The Countryside Commission is the Government agency responsible for, among many other things, the National Parks in England and Wales, each of which produces extensive literature of its own, including an invaluable handbook guide to what each National Park has to offer.

*Crossing, W., <u>Western Morning Post Guide to Dartmoor</u>, 1909 and 1912.

*Docharty, W.McKnight, <u>A Selection of Some 900 British and Irish Mountain Tops</u>, (privately), 1954

*Docharty, W.McKnight, <u>The Supplement to A Selection of Some 900 British and Irish Mountain Tops;   and A Selection of 1,000 Tops Under 2,500 Feet</u> (privately), 1962. 2 vols.

*Elmslie, W.T., <u>The Two Thousand Footers of England</u>, The Journal of the

Fell and Rock Climbing Club of the English Lake District, 1933, pp 344-351.

*Evans, H.M., and Thomas, W.O., <u>Y Geiriadur Mawr: The Complete Welsh-English, English-Welsh Dictionary</u>, Llyfrau'r Dryw a Gwasg Aberystwyth.

Forestry Commission; 25 Saville Row, London, WIX 2AY.   Various publications including handbooks to the National Forest Parks.

Jaffa, G., A Rambler's Guide to County Names, "Climber & Rambler" magazine, George Outram & Co. Ltd., 1971 October, pp 340-341.

*McWhirter, N., and McWhirter, R., <u>Guinness Book of Records</u>, Guinness Superlatives Ltd., 1971, p 57 (County Tops).

*Moss, E., <u>The Two-Thousands of England (Excluding the Lake District)</u> Rucksack Club Journal, 1939, pp 184-189.

*Moss, E., <u>The Two-Thousands of Wales</u>, Rucksack Club Journal, 1940, pp 239-243.

*Moss, E., <u>The County Tops of England and Wales</u>, Rucksack Club Journal, 1951, pp 319-327.

*Moss, E., <u>All Those Two-Thousands</u>, Rucksack Club Journal, 1952, pp 67-70.

Mountain Rescue Committee;   9 Milldale Avenue, Temple Meads, Buxton. <u>Mountain Rescue and Cave Rescue</u>, Handbook of First Aid in British Mountains, and Rescue Posts, etc., 1972.

Munro, Sir Hugh T., (revised by Donaldson, J.C., and Coats, W.L.) <u>Munro's Tables of the 3000-Feet Mountains of Scotland, and Other Tables of Lesser Heights</u>, Scottish Mountaineering Trust, 1969.

Neill, J., and Elfyn Hughes, R., <u>The Names of Crags in Snowdonia</u>, Climbers' Club Journal, 1964, pp 172-184.

*Neill, J., and Elfyn Hughes, R., <u>The Names of Crags in Snowdonia</u>, Climbers' Club Journal, 1965, pp 259-276.

Pearsall, W.H., <u>Mountains and Moorland</u>,   Collins New Naturalist Series, 1950.

Periodicals; "Climber & Rambler", see under Jaffa, G. Climbers' Club Journal, see under Neill, J. Fell & Rock Club Journal, see under Elmslie, W.T. Rucksack Club Journal, see under Moss, E., and Rooke Corbett, J. Wayfarers' Journal, see under Simpson, F.H.F.

Poucher, W.A., The Lakeland Peaks, Constable & Co. Ltd., 1962.

Poucher, W.A., The Peaks and Pennines, Constable & Co. Ltd., 1966.

Poucher, W.A., The Welsh Peaks, Constable & Co. Ltd., 1970.

   And also other books on British mountains.

*Pyatt, E.C., and Clark, R.W., Mountaineering in Britain: A History from the Earliest Times to the Present Day, Phoenix House Ltd., 1957. Many references, especially pp 215-226.

Pyatt, E.C., Where to Climb in the British Isles, Faber & Faber, 1960.

Pyatt, E.C., Mountains of Britain, B.T. Batsford, 1966. And also several other works on aspects of British climbing and hill-walking.

Ramblers' Association; 1/4 Crawford Mews, London, WIH 1PT. Various publications of interest to all outdoor people.

*Rooke Corbett, J., Twenty-Fives, Rucksack Club Journal, 1911, pp 61-65.

*Rooke Corbett, J., Twenty-Fives, Rucksack Club Journal, 1929, pp 337-344.

Rowland, E.G., Hill Walking in Snowdonia, Cidron Press, 1970.

*Simpson, F.H.F., Concerning Contours, Wayfarers' Journal, 1937, 18-24. A list of the two-thousanders of the Lake District.

Stamp, L. Dudley, Britain's Structure and Scenery, Collins New Naturalist Series, 1960.

*Wainwright, A., A Pictorial Guide to the Lakeland Fells, Westmorland Gazette Ltd. Book One: The Eastern Fells, 1955. Book Two: The Far Eastern Fells, 1957. Book Three: The Central Fells, 1958. Book Four: The Southern Fells, 1960. Book Five: The Northern Fells, 1962. *Book Six: The North Western Fells, 1964. *Book Seven: The Western Fells, 1966.

Wainwright, A., <u>Pennine Way Companion</u>, Westmorland Gazette, 1968.

Wainwright, A., <u>Walks in Limestone Country</u>, Westmorland Gazette Ltd., n.d. (1970). Largely concerned with the Craven district of Yorkshire (Whernside, Ingleborough and Penyghent).

Young, G. Winthrop, <u>Mountain Craft</u>, Methuen & Co. Ltd., 1920 (and later editions including 1949). The classic instructional handbook for mountaineering.

Youth Hostels Association (England and Wales); 8 St. Stephen's Hill, St. Albans, Herts. Various publications of interest to outdoor people, including a handbook of the 260 hostels, in England and Wales, most of which are in mountain or hill country.

GLOSSARY OF WELSH MOUNTAIN NAMES

Aderyn; adar	bird; birds
Adwy	gap, pass
Afon	river
Allt, Gallt	hillside, cliff
Amarch	dishonour?
Aran	high place, eminence
Ardd	hill, height
Ardudwy	District in which lies the Rhinog range of mountains
Arennig	(?)
Arwystli	(?)
Bach, Fach	1. small, little, lesser;
	2. nook, corner
Bala	outlet of a lake
Ban, Fan; Bannau	peak, beacon; peaks, beacons
Bangor	monastery originally covered of wattle rods
Bedd	grave
Ben	waggon, cart; head
Benglog	skull
Benllyn, Penllyn	head of a lake; an ancient cantref (hundred or district) at head of Llyn Tegid, Bala Lake.
Bera	rick, stack, pyramid
Berfedd, Perfedd	middle, entrails
Berwyn	foaming?; passion? (Berw = a rush of water)
Betws	chapel, oratory
Beudy	shippen
Blaen; Blaenau	end, edge, source, extreme; extremes, upper reaches
Bleiddiau	young wolves
Bochgen	(?) (Boch = cheek)
Boeth, Poeth	warm, hot, burnt
Boncyn, Boncen, Poncyn, Poncen	small hillock
Bont, Pont	bridge
Borth, Porth	gate, harbour
Braich	ridge, spur
Brenin	king
Brith	speckled, coarse
Bron, Fron	hill-breast
Bronwen	white-breasted
Brwynog	rushy, marshy

Brych	speckled
Brycheiniog	Brecknock, Brecknockshire
Bryn	hill
Bustach	bullock
Bwch	buck
Bwlch	gap, pass, col, notch
Bwrdd	table, board
Bychan, Fechan	little, tiny

Cadair, Gadair	seat, chair
Cader, Gader	stronghold
Cader Idris	chair of Idris. According to legend, Idris was a warrior killed at a battle on the banks of the River Severn about the year A.D. 630.
Cae	field, enclosure
Caer, Gaer	stronghold, fort
Caerfyrddin	Carmarthenshire
Caernarfon	Caernarvon(shire)
Cafn	trough
Calch	lime, chalk
Capel	chapel
Carn, Garn; Carnau, Garnau	cairn, tumulus, burial-mound
Carnedd, Garnedd; Carneddau, Garneddau, Carneddi	cairn, tumulus, burial-mound; cairns, burial-mounds
Carreg; Cerrig	stone, rock; stones, rocks
Carw	deer, stag
Caseg	mare
Castell	castle, small stronghold, imposing natural position
Cau	hollow, concave enclosed valley, shut in
Cefn	ridge
Ceredigion	Cardiganshire
Cerrig, Cerig	stones, rocks
Ceunant	ravine, gorge
Chwarel	quarry
Ci; Cŵn	dog; dogs
Cil	recess, retreat
Cidwm	wolf
Clip	precipice, crag, steep slope, bluff
Clogwyn	cliff
Clwyd	hurdle, gate

Clyd	sheltered
Clwyedog	sensed?
Cnicht	probably from Middle English Cnight = knight, from the bascinet helmet-shape of the peak (Moel Siabod Group).
Coch, Goch	red
Coed	wood
Condryll	shattered
Corn	peak, horn-shaped summit
Cors	swamp
Cowarch	(?)
Cowlyd	grey thread?
Craf	garlic
Craig, Graig; Creigiau	rock, crag, cliff; rocks, crags
Crib, Grib, Cribin, Gribin	crest, serrated summit ridge
Croes, Groes	cross
Crug, Grug	heap or mound
Cwellyn	basket?
Cwm	coomb, valley head (cymoedd = plural of cwm)
Cŵn	dogs (Ci = dog)
Cyfrwy	ridge between two summits, saddle
Cyfyng	narrows, straits
Cynghorion	advice, councel
Cyrniau	cones, cairns
Cywion	chickens (young grouse?)
Dafydd, Carnedd Dafydd	Mountain summit apparently named after the brother of the last native Prince of Wales, Llywelyn, (q. v.).
Daren	(Darren = hill)
Ddafad	sheep, ewe. Also: Dafad
Ddelw, Delw	image
Ddol, Dol	meadow
Dduallt	black spur, black cliff
Ddysgl, Dysgl	dish. Crib-y-ddysgl (Snowdon Group) may = the ridge shaped like the edge of a dish or bowl
Diffwys	precipice, abyss
Dinas, Ddinas	fortress, city, prominent natural position
Dinbych	Denbighshire
Diocyn	(?)
Dirion	(?)
Dringarth	(?) (Dring = ascent; Dringwr = climber; Arth = bear)
Drosgl, Drosgyl	rough hill? (Dros = over)

Drum, Trum	ridge
Druman	(?)
Drws	gap, narrow pass, door
Drygarn	(?)
Du, ddu, duon	black, dark
Dulas	dark stream
Duwynt	(?)
Dŵr, Dwfr	water
Dy, Tŷ	house
Dyffryn	valley
Dywarchen, Tywarchen	turf

Eglwys	church
Eigiau	deep?; shoals of fish
Eilio	to second, to plait, to weave, to compose
Elen	fawn, young deer
Elidir	According to legend, the mountain summit in the Glyders Group was given this name to commemmorate a north-country Briton, Elidir Mwynfawr, who claimed the government of North Wales and was slain at Abermweddus, near Clynnog, a place which cannot now be identified.
Eryri, Eryri Fawr	the high land; the mountains of central Snowdonia especially those of the Snowdon, Glyders and Carneddau groups.
Erw	acre
Esgair	long ridge, spur

Fach, Bach	small, little, lesser
Faen, Maen	stone
Fagl	(Bagl = a crutch)
Fammau	(?)
Fan, Ban	peak, beacon
Fawddwy, Mawddwy	an ancient cantref (hundred or district) in Merionethshire
Fawn, Mawn; Fawnog, Mawnog	peat bog; peaty
Fawr, Mawr	big, great, greater
Fechan, Bychan	small, tiny
Felen, Melyn	yellow
Fferna	(?)
Fflint	Flint, Flintshire
Fforchog	forked, forked streams
Ffordd	road
Ffridd	mountain enclosure, sheep-walk

Ffynnon, Ffynon	spring, well
Fign, Figyn, Mign, Siglen	bog
Filiast, Miliast	greyhound bitch
Foel, Moel	bare hill
Fras	(?)
Fron, Bron	hill-breast, rounded hill
Fynydd, Mynydd	mountain, moorland
Gadair, Gader	seat, chair
Gaer, Caer	fort
Gallt, Allt	hillside, cliff
Gafr; Geifr	goat; goats
Gareg, Garreg	stone, rock, crag
Garn	rock, cairn
Garnedd, Carnedd	cairn, tumulus, burial-mound
Garth	promontory, hill enclosure
Garw	coarse, rough
Gelli	grove, copse
Gihirych	(?)
Glan, Lan	shore, river-bank, hillock
Glas, Lâs; Gleision	1. grey, green, blue 2. brook
Glasgwm	green valley-head?
Gleisiad	young salmon
Gleision	whey
Glyder (= Y Gludair)	pile of rocks, "cairn"
Glyn	valley, glen
Goch, Coch	red
Godor	hindrance, delay?
Gogof, Ogof, Ogo	cave, lair
Gorffwysfa, Gorphwysfa	resting-place
Gorllwyn	ambush
Gornach	(?)
Gorsedd	cairn, tumulus, burial-mound
Grach	scrabby
Graeanog	gravelly
Graig, Craig; Creigiau	rock, crag; crags
Grib, Crib, Gribin, Cribin	ridge crest, serrated summit ridge

194

Gris; Grisiau	step; steps
Groes, Croes	cross
Gron	(Cron = round)
Gwaen	(?)
Gwalch	hawk
Gwaun, Waun	moor, mountain meadow, moorland field
Gwên, Gwyn	white
Gwern	swamp, place where alders grow (grew)
Gwrâch, Wrâch	hag, witch
Gwryd	fathom
Gwyddfa, Wyddfa	cairn, tumulus, burial-mound. (see also Y Wyddfa).
Gwyliwr	watchman; perhaps also upstanding stone resembling a man on a hill summit
Gwyn, Gwên	white
Gwynant	(?)
Gwynedd	North-West Wales
Gwynt; Gwyntog	wind; windy
Gylchedd	(?)
Hafod	summer dwelling (farm)
Hafoty, Hafodty	summer dwelling (farm)
Hebog	hawk, falcon
Helen (Elen, Y Leng)	Sarn Helen - road or causeway of the legion. See also Sarn.
Helgi-du	black hound, black hunting-dog
Helyg	willows
Hên	old
Hendre, Hendref	winter dwelling, old house (farm)
Hir	long
Hirnant	long valley
Hydd	stag
Hyll	ugly
Hywel	Howell (personal name)
Iago	James
Idris	Idris (see Cader Idris)
Ifan	John
Isaf	lower, lowest
Lâs, Glas	green, blue, grey
Lefn, Llefn	smooth
Llan	church, parish, village, enclosure

Llanerch	glade
Llangynidr	(?)
Llech	slate, stone slab
Llechog	slaty
Llechwedd	hillside
Lledr	leather; wide, broad
Llefn, Lefn	smooth
Llethr	slope, slabs?
Llia	(?)
Llithrig	slippery
Lliwedd	stained or coloured
Lloer	moon
Lluest	hut, bothy
Llugwy	bright stream
Llwybr	path
Llwyd, Lwyd	grey, brown
Llŵyn; Llŵyni	bush; bushes
Llwytmor	(?)
Llyfn	smooth
Llyfnant	(?)
Llygad	eye; source of a river or stream
Llyn; Llynnau or Llynnoedd	lake; lakes
Llysiau	herbs
Llywelyn, Carnedd Llywelyn	Mountain summit apparently named after Llywelyn, 1194-1240, the last native Prince of Wales. See also Dafydd.

Maen, Faen	stone
Maes, Faes	open field, plain
Maesglasau	(?)
Maesyfed	Radnorshire
Main	1. thin, narrow 2. (as Maen) stone
Manod	fine snow, driven snow
March; Meirch	horse, stallion; horses
Marian	moraine
Mawddwy, Fawddwy	(see Fawddwy)
Mawn, Fawn; Mawnog	peat bog; peaty
Mawr, Fawr	big, great, greater
Meirionydd	Merionethshire
Melyn, Felen	yellow

Mign, Fign Siglen	bog, morass, quagmire
Mignedd	bogs, quagmires
Migneint	boggy district
Miliast, Filiast	greyhound bitch
Mochyn; Moch	pig; pigs
Moel, Foel	bare hill-top
Moelwyn	white hill?
Môn, Sir Fôn	Anglesey
Morgannwg	Glamorgan
Mot	the name of a legendary giant. In Snowdonia the name is often given to a sheepdog
Mur	wall
Mwyn	ore, mine
Mynwy	Monmouthshire; (River) Monnow
Mynydd, Fynydd	mountain, moorland. (Mynydd-dir = hill-country; Mynyddog = mountainous; Mynyddwr = mountaineer)
Nant	brook, ravine, valley
Nedd	nits, lice
Niwl	mist, hill-fog
Nôd	aim, mark, boss
Oer	cold, exposed
Ogof, Ogo, Gogof	cave, lair
Oleu-wen	white light; moonlight?
Pair	cauldron; perhaps also bubbling spring
Pant	hollow, valley, cwm
Pen, Ben	head, top, end, edge, summit
Penamnen	(?)
Penfro	Pembrokeshire
Pennant	head of a glen
Penolau	(?)
Perfedd, Berfedd	middle, entrails
Person	person, parson
Picws	oatcake
Pistyll	spout, waterfall
Poeth, Boeth	warm, hot, burnt
Poncen, Poncyn, Boncen, Boncyn	small hillock
Pont, Bont	bridge

Porth, Borth	gate, gateway, harbour
Pumlumon	(?) (Anglicised in the past as "Plynlimon")
Pwll	pit, pool, hollow
Pydew	pit, well

Rhaeadr	waterfall (Anglicised in the past as "Rhayader")
Rhedyn	bracken
Rhinog	secret? (Rhiniog = narrow pass, threshold)
Rhiw	hill, slope, ascent
Rhobell	(?)
Rhos	moor, promontory
Rhudd	red, crimson
Rhyd	ford

Saeth	arrow
Sarn	causeway, pavement, stepping-stones
Siabod	possibly from Middle English schabbed = scabbed
Siglen	morass
Silyn	(Silin = spawn)
Sir	shire, county
Snowdon; Snowdonia	snow-peak; snow-peak country. The names occur quite early: Old English Snawdune, Middle English Snaudon and Snaudonia. See also Y Wyddfa.
Stac	(?)
Sych	dry

Tâl	front, end
Tan	under, as far as
Tarren	knoll, rocky tump
Tarw	bull
Teg	fair, beautiful
Tegid	beautiful
Tomle	(dung-heap?)
Traws, Draws	across, yonder
Trefaldwyn	Montgomery(shire)
Trefeilw	(?)
Trum, Drum	ridge
Tryfan (more correctly, Y Tryfan)	The Mountain which rises very high and steeply, or which has a sharp or narrow or finger-like summit.
Tumpa	knoll? (Twmpath = tump, knoll)
Twr; Tyrau	tower; towers
Twyn	hillock, knoll

| Tŷ, Dy | house |
| Tyrau | towers |

| Uchaf | higher, highest |
| Ugain | twenty. Carnedd Ugain on Crib-y-ddysgl (Snowdon Group); also known locally as Carnedd Ddigin. |

Waen	(?)
Waun, Gwaun	moor, mountain meadow, moorland field
Wen, Gwên, Gwyn	white
Wenallt	white hillside
Wrâch, Gwrâch	hag, witch
Wyddfa	cairn, tumulus, burial-mound. See Y Wyddfa.
Wyn	white

Y, Yr, 'r	the (or in effect, of the)
Yn, Ym	in
Ysbytty, Ysbyty	hospice, hospital
Ysfa	sheep-walk
Ysgafell	ledge, brow
Ysgol; Ysgolion	step; 1. ladders, 2. school
Ysgyfarnogod	hares, possessing hares
Ystrad	valley, strath, river-meadow
Ystwyth	winding, bending
Y Wyddfa	the tumulus or tomb. In the legend, the giant Rhita Gawr, killed by King Arthur, was buried in the summit cairn at the top of Snowdon. The summit has also been known as Gwyddfa Rhita and Carnedd y Cawr (Cairn of the Giant). The form Yr Wyddfa on the present O.S. maps appears to be incorrect.

READER'S LOGBOOK

Date	Time		Companions	Weather
	start	finish		

Peaks Ascended

READER'S LOGBOOK

Date	Time		Companions	Weather
	start	finish		

Peaks Ascended

READER'S LOGBOOK

Date	Time		Companions	Weather
	start	finish		

Peaks Ascended

READER'S LOGBOOK

Date	Time		Companions	Weather
	start	finish		
	start	finish		

Peaks Ascended

READER'S LOGBOOK

Date	Time		Companions	Weather
	start	finish		

Peaks Ascended

READER'S LOGBOOK

Date	Time		Companions	Weather
	start	finish		

Peaks Ascended

READER'S LOGBOOK

Date	Time		Companions	Weather
	start	finish		
	start	finish		

Peaks Ascended

READER'S LOGBOOK

Date	Time		Companions	Weather
	start	finish		
	start	finish		

Peaks Ascended

READER'S LOGBOOK

Date	Time		Companions	Weather
	start	finish		

READER'S LOGBOOK

Date	Time		Companions	Weather
	start	finish		

Peaks Ascended

READER'S LOGBOOK

Date	Time		Companions	Weather
	start	finish		
Date	Time		Companions	Weather
	start	finish		

Peaks Ascended

READER'S LOGBOOK

Date	Time		Companions	Weather
	start	finish		
	start	finish		

Peaks Ascended